OCS Study
MMS 2001-019

Coastal Marine Institute

Lafourche Parish and Port Fourchon, Louisiana: Effects of the Outer Continental Shelf Petroleum Industry on the Economy and Public Services, Part 1

U.S. Department of the Interior
Minerals Management Service
Gulf of Mexico OCS Region

Cooperative Agreement
Coastal Marine Institute
Louisiana State University

OCS Study
MMS 2001-019

Coastal Marine Institute

Lafourche Parish and Port Fourchon, Louisiana: Effects of the Outer Continental Shelf Petroleum Industry on the Economy and Public Services, Part 1

Author

Diane C. Keithly

May 2001

Prepared under MMS Contract
14-35-0001-30660-19945
by
Coastal Marine Institute
Louisiana State University
Baton Rouge, Louisiana 70801

Published by

U.S. Department of the Interior
Minerals Management Service
Gulf of Mexico OCS Region

Cooperative Agreement
Coastal Marine Institute
Louisiana State University

DISCLAIMER

This report was prepared under contract between the Minerals Management Service (MMS) and the Louisiana State University, Coastal Marine Institute. This report has been technically reviewed by the MMS, and it has been approved for publication. Approval does not signify that the contents necessarily reflect the views and policies of the MMS, nor does mention of trade names or commercial products constitute endorsement or recommendation for use. It is, however, exempt from review and compliance with the MMS editorial standards.

REPORT AVAILABILITY

Extra copies of this report may be obtained from the Public Information Office (Mail Stop 5034) at the following address:

U.S. Department of the Interior
Minerals Management Service
Gulf of Mexico OCS Region
Public Information Office (MS 5034)
1201 Elmwood Park Boulevard
New Orleans, LA 70123-2394

Telephone: 504-736-2519 or 1-800-200-GULF

CITATION

Suggested citation:

Keithly, D. C. 2001. Lafourche Parish and Port Fourchon, Louisiana: Effects of the Outer Continental Shelf Petroleum Industry on the Economy and Public Services, Part 1. OCS Study MMS 2001-019. Prepared by the Louisiana State University, Coastal Marine Institute. U.S. Department of the Interior, Minerals Management Service, Gulf of Mexico OCS Region, New Orleans, LA. 23 pp.

TABLE OF CONTENTS

LIST OF FIGURES

LIST OF TABLES

Introduction

Port Fourchon, Louisiana's only port directly adjacent to the Gulf of Mexico, is located on the coast of Lafourche Parish. The port is strategically positioned to serve industrial activity associated with the exploration and development of the vast oil and gas resources, which lie beneath the Gulf. Although a relatively young port when compared with ports such as New Orleans or Galveston, Port Fourchon is growing at a visible rate due to increasing oil and gas development on the Outer Continental Shelf.

As pictured below in Figure 1, the port was established in 1960 during the administration of Governor Jimmy Davis. Under the leadership of State Senator A.O. Rappelet and other local gubernatorial appointees, Port Fourchon was identified as the "Port of the Future" for fishing, oil and gas activity, and foreign trade. A significant boost to the development of the port also took place in the 1960s when the people of the tenth ward of Lafourche Parish voted to tax themselves to fund the port. In 1970, the first elected commission took office and elected Nolty Theriot its president. Theriot was a local businessman and community leader who also had experience in international oil exploration and development. He and other commissioners saw early on the tremendous potential of Port Fourchon (Falgout, personal interview, 1999).

Figure 1. Governor Davis Signing Port Legislation. Pictured are (left to right) State Representative Wollen Falgout, State Senator A.O. Rappelet, Governor Jimmy Davis, and State Representative Dudley Bernard.

The Growth of the Port

Two companies had located on port property by 1978. As of August 1999, 124 companies are located there. Leasing activity has been particularly brisk in recent years due to increased offshore oil and gas activity on the Outer Continental Shelf. For example, there were 50 lessees and 113 businesses in June, 1998; less than a year later in May, 1999 there were 54 lessees and 124 businesses. In other words, new businesses located at the port at the rate of one per month (Greater Lafourche Port Commission Mailing List, June 24, 1998 and May 21, 1999). Table 1 below shows the growth from 1990-1998, and Figure 2 depicts graphically the rates of growth.

The physical size of the port has grown from about 25 acres in 1980 to nearly 600 acres today. Figure 3 shows the strategic location of the port relative to the Gulf of Mexico. Total waterfront at the port has increased from less than 5,000 feet in 1980 to nearly 25,000 feet. Much of the increase has taken place in the last five years. For example, the developed acreage at the port nearly doubled from 1992 to 1997. The waterfront also roughly doubled in this five-year period. And the port is growing still; a multimillion-dollar contract was awarded in late 1998 to expand the port. Further, the entire area to be added is already committed to leases, according to Executive Director Ted Falgout.

Port Fourchon is a multi-use port servicing the needs of oil and gas development, commercial fishing, recreation, and shipping as well as serving as the land base for the Louisiana Offshore Port Authority (LOOP). However, much of the increase in economic activity associated with the port in the past five years is due to the growth of oil and gas development in deepwater areas of the Gulf of Mexico. (Deepwater oil and gas wells are those found in water with a depth in excess of 1,000 feet.)

Table 1: Port Fourchon Leases, Acreage, and Waterfront Growth - 1990-1998

Year	Leases	Acreage	Waterfront (feet)
1990	18	105	6,499
1991	23	122	8,691
1992	26	149	12,344
1993	27	151	12,896
1994	37	187	18,123
1995	45	211	19,162
1996	56	249	21,154
1997	75	338	26,542
1998	85	417	33,505

Source: Greater Lafourche Port Commission (June, 1999).

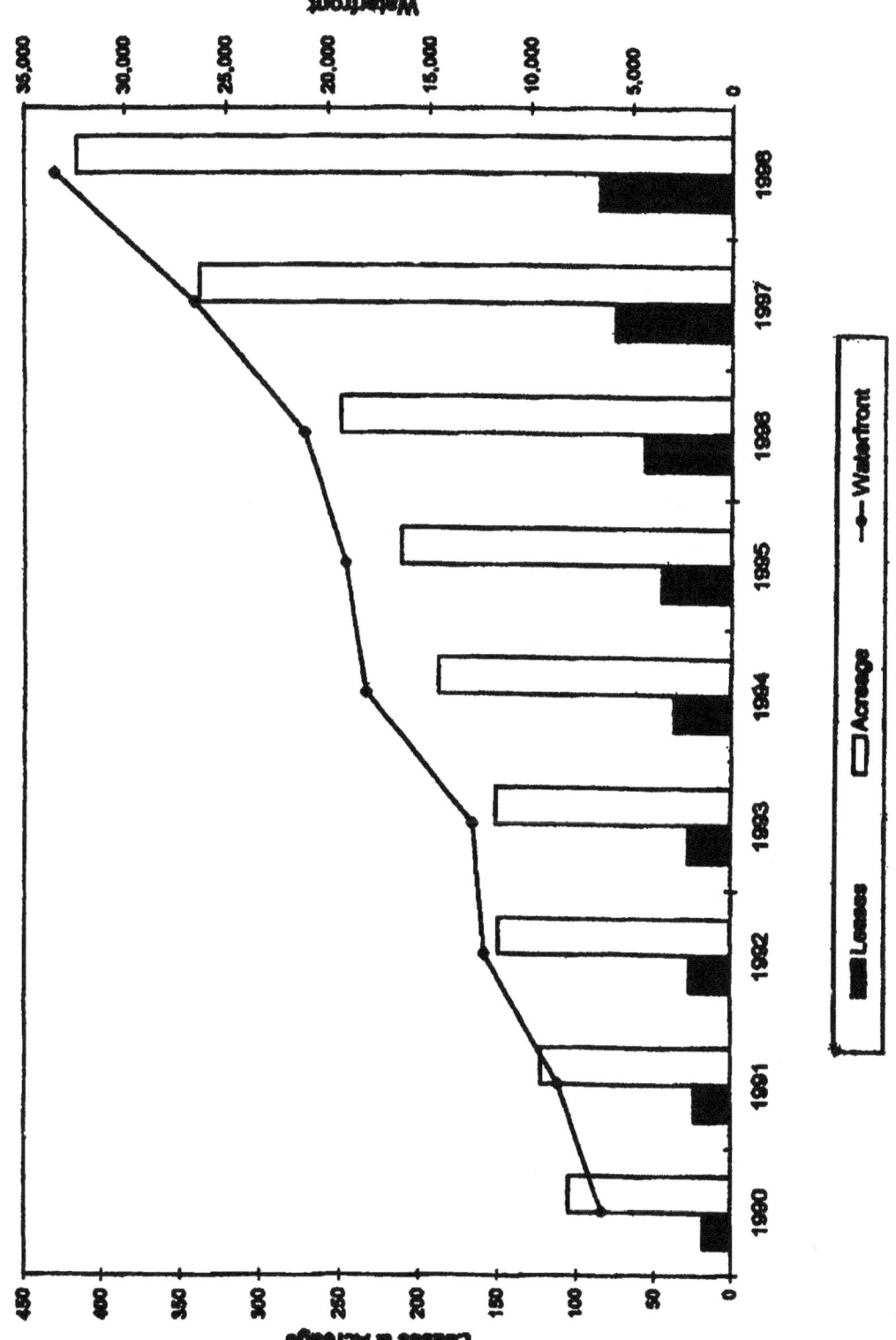

Source: Greater Lafourche Port Commission (June 1999).

Figure 2. Greater Lafourche Port Commission Leases, Acreage and Waterfront Growth, 1990-1998.

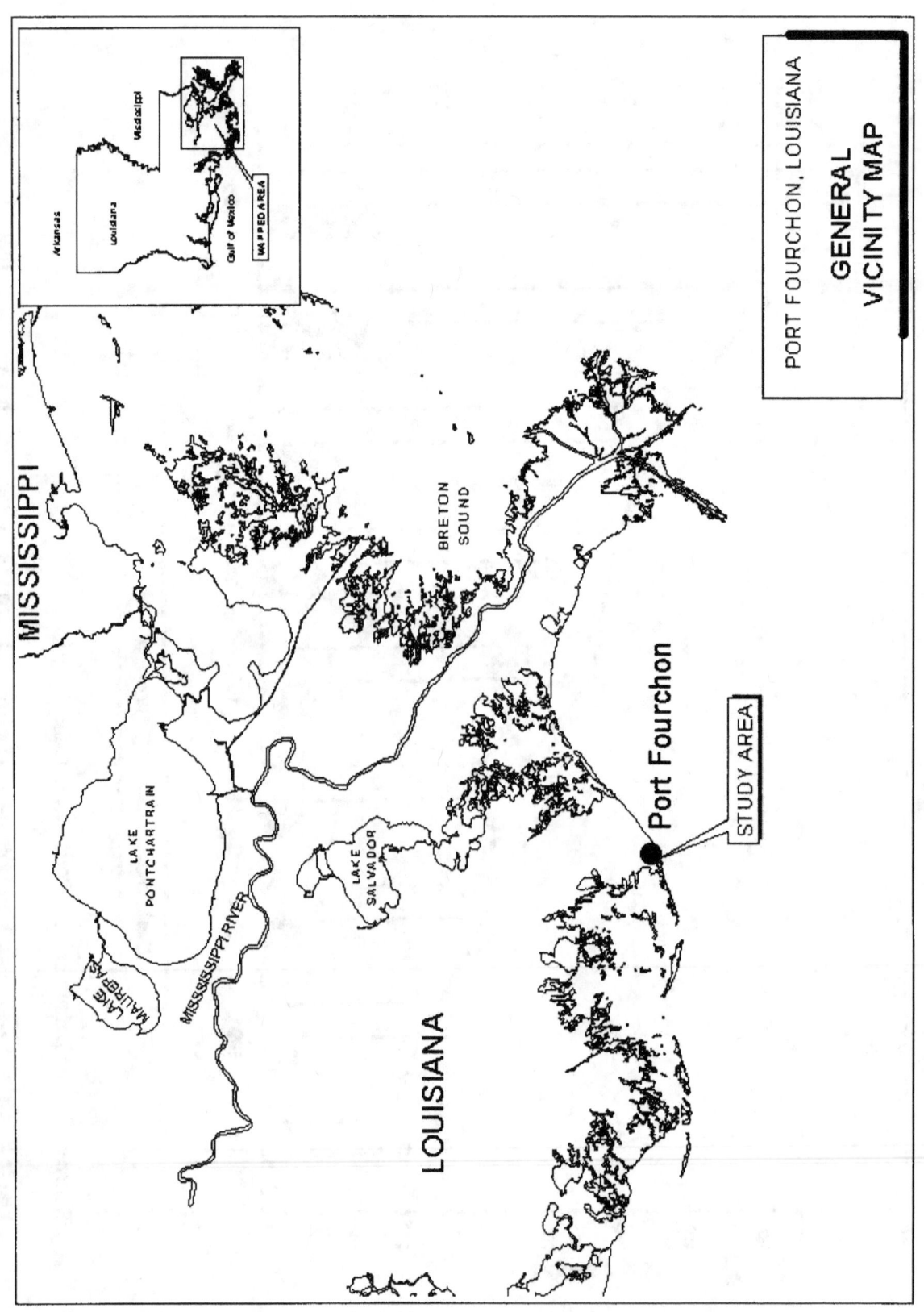

Figure 3. Port Fourchon, Louisiana's Only Port Located Directly on the Gulf of Mexico.

The types of businesses located at the port vary. The largest group is businesses involved in offshore oil and gas support services (43.6%). A distant second in number are those involved directly in oil and gas exploration (11.3%). The remaining group includes businesses involved in commercial fishing, recreation, research, retail sales, construction, communication, drilling, environmental services, and technical services. In addition, one public agency and the Louisiana Offshore Oil Port (LOOP) are located at the port. See Tables 2, 3, and 4 for details.

Table 2: Types of Businesses Located at Port Fourchon (May 21, 1999)

Type of Business	Frequency
Commercial Fishing	2 (1.6%)
Communication	1 (0.8%)
Construction	3 (2.4%)
Drilling	8 (6.5%)
Environmental	9 (7.3%)
Oil and Gas	14 (11.3%)
Offshore Port*	1 (0.8%)
Public Agency	1 (0.8%)
Public Lodging	1 (0.8%)
Recreation (includes recreational fishing)	5 (4%)
Research	1 (0.8%)
Retail	7 (5.7%)
Support Services	54 (43.6%)
Technical	5 (4%)
Transportation	12 (9.7%)
TOTAL	**124**

* LOOP, only offshore port in the U.S.

Table 3: Daily Average Number and Total Number of Vessels
at Port Fourchon by Type, January 1998 - December 1998.

	Fishing Boat	Supply	Crew Boat	Recreational	Tank Barge	Tugboat
January 1998						
Sum	838	1405	786	121	207	622
Avg	27	45	25	4	7	20
February 1998						
Sum	1062	1461	721	138	9	548
Avg	38	52	26	5	0	20
March 1998						
Sum	953	1619	1299	148	12	579
Avg	31	52	42	5	0	19
April 1998						
Sum	861	1578	1008	172	27	545
Avg	29	53	34	6	1	18
May 1998						
Sum	560	1559	1012	386	53	685
Avg	18	50	33	13	2	22
June 1998						
Sum	673	1517	980	306	99	518
Avg	23	52	34	11	3	18
July 1998						
Sum	815	1601	949	433	127	550
Avg	26	52	31	14	4	18
August 1998						
Sum	805	1553	907	391	124	577
Avg	26	50	29	13	4	19
September 1998						
Sum	831	1789	873	306	160	475
Avg	28	60	29	10	5	16
October 1998						
Sum	759	1500	891	302	157	492
Avg	24	48	29	10	5	16
November 1998						
Sum	737	1613	1020	247	118	550
Avg	25	54	34	8	4	18
December 1998						
Sum	834	1858	1027	274	137	813
Avg	27	60	33	9	4	20
Grand Total	9728	19053	11473	3224	1230	6754

Source: Greater Lafourche Parish Port Commission (June 1999).

Table 4: Daily Average Number and Total Number of Vessels
at Port Fourchon by Type, January 1999 - May 1999.

	Fishing Boat	Supply	Crew Boat	Recreational	Tank Barge	Tugboat
January 1999						
Sum	971	1791	983	281	125	663
Avg	31	58	32	9	4	21
February 1999						
Sum	814	1781	768	245	126	631
Avg	29	64	27	9	5	23
March 1999						
Sum	902	1755	939	316	162	760
Avg	29	57	30	10	5	25
April 1999						
Sum	829	1720	737	467	235	456
Avg	28	57	25	16	8	15
May 1999						
Sum	690	1733	1017	451	166	657
Avg	22	56	33	15	5	21
Grand Total	4206	8780	4444	1760	814	3167

Source: Greater Lafourche Parish Port Commission (June 1999).

A Brief History of Offshore Oil and Gas Development

Offshore oil and gas development began in 1933 when wells were drilled off the coasts of California and Louisiana. The first well in the Gulf of Mexico was located about one mile off the coast in 13 feet of water. Fifteen years later the first well off Louisiana's coast and beyond the sight of land was completed and producing 600 barrels of oil per day. During this early period onshore support for offshore activity began to develop along the coast. Drilling activity continued to move farther offshore, and by the mid-1950s wells 50 miles offshore were common. As oil and gas activity in the Gulf of Mexico grew so did onshore support facilities such as oil-field equipment dealers, air transport services, marine equipment companies, and services for engineering and contract labor.

After nearly a half century of production in the Gulf of Mexico it appeared to many that the area was nearly spent and had no long-term future in oil and gas development. By the 1980s the Gulf was humorously referred to as the "dead sea." This quickly changed when new discoveries were made in the Gulf's deepwater areas during the 1990s. Eleven deepwater discoveries were made in 1998 alone. In 1995, new Federal legislation, the OCS Deepwater Royalty Relief Act, stimulated business development in offshore oil and gas activity. In addition, new technological developments in exploration substantially lowered the costs of recovering oil and gas resources in the deepwater of the Gulf. All the aforementioned factors brought about a marked revival of oil and gas activity on the Outer Continental Shelf (OCS) and a tremendous growth in the need for onshore support.

In 1990, deepwater oil production in the Gulf of Mexico totaled 12 million barrels representing four percent of the total Gulf output; in 1996, the figure had risen to 63 million barrels representing 17% of the total. Melancon and Roby (1998) project that the proportion of output from deepwater wells in the Gulf will rise to the range of 54 to 64% by the end of 2000. In the span of a decade, the Gulf of Mexico went from being termed the "dead sea" to being referred to as "America's new frontier" (Cranswick and Regg, 1997).

Another indication of the growth of oil and gas activity is the rise in the number of permits to drill in the deepwater of the Gulf of Mexico. In 1992, the Minerals Management Service granted 39 permits; in 1996, the number of permits totaled 126. Further, the number of fields with proven reserves increased from 15 in 1992 to 25 in 1996. Finally, production from deepwater fields rose 40% in the first seven months of 1997 over the level of the same period in the preceding year (Langely, et al., 1998).

In the last 18 months the industry slumped somewhat in Louisiana. The Louisiana Department of Labor reported that the oil and gas industry lost 4,800 jobs between May 1998 and May 1999; in Houma, Louisiana, approximately 50 miles from Port Fourchon, 1600 industry jobs were lost. Rig counts, the number of drilling rigs under contract, in the state declined from a high of 219 in December 1997 to a low of 121 in April 1999. However, the downturn may be short-lived. According to LSU economist Loren Scott, the downturn has already reversed as indicated by the rig count which rose to 140 in June 1999. Increases in the price of oil have helped to create more business activity (Griggs, 1999).

According to The Greater Baton Rouge Business Report (July 6-July 19, 1999) (Turk, 1999) the downturn did not deal a serious setback to the industry as in the mid-1980s for a variety of reasons. Technology, such as 3-D seismic technology and enhanced completion and horizontal drilling techniques, has allowed the industry to realize a profit at lower oil prices. Further, oil prices are rising and the price of natural gas has been fairly stable. In addition, natural gas in the Gulf of Mexico is produced and used in North America and, therefore, is not subject to changes in the global economy (Turk, 1999).

A study of oil and gas production projections in the Gulf of Mexico published earlier this year reported that the recent downturn in activity lead to decreased bidding on leases, but the study also noted that interest in areas over 800 meters (about 2600 feet) deep remained strong. The number of bids for these areas was just under 50 in 1994, over 1,000 in 1997, and over 800 in 1998 (Melancon and Baud, 1999).

Port Fourchon and Deepwater OCS Development

According to Roger White, director of business development for Edison Chouest Offshore, major American and foreign oil companies are moving more and more into the development of deepwater areas because the return on investment is greater than for land or nearshore facilities. Port Fourchon is one of the few ports in the Gulf of Mexico equipped to handle the needs of deepwater oil and gas development. According to White, Port Fourchon is the most reasonable place, considering time and distance, for many companies to use since it is in closest proximity to a great deal of deepwater development. Other river ports in Louisiana that can accommodate deepwater vessels have the disadvantage of their more inland locations; other ports in the Gulf of Mexico region, such as Galveston or Mobile, are too distant. Further, foreign companies are attracted to the Gulf over other areas of the world because it offers political stability.

Port Fourchon also has a unique advantage in that the port has the only facility in the world that can service deepwater supply vessels as pictured in Figure 4. The channel depth allows these vessels to take on fuel, water, deck cargo, barites, cements, liquid muds, and completion fluids efficiently at the same covered dock. According to White, normally such servicing would be done at more than one dock and could take a full 48 to 72 hours. Because these vessels represent significant business investments, their more efficient use is an important competitive advantage. This one-stop-shopping facility, called C-Port, has cut vessel turnaround time by more than 50% (see Figure 5). An additional facility is under construction and a third one is planned at the port, shown in Figure 6.

White sees benefits for the entire nation in the development of deepwater oil and gas activity in the Gulf of Mexico. The nation as a whole will become less dependent on foreign supplies and the efficiency that Port Fourchon offers the industry will be reflected in lower prices for consumers. There also benefits for the state and the local community according to White, but along with these benefits come some costs that the state and particularly the local community must bear (White, personal interview, 1999).

Impacts on the Local Community

White mentions the inadequate infrastructure of the local area. He says that not only is the poor road access to the port going to stymie development, but also it is a burden for local citizens. Louisiana Highway 1 is the only land access to the port. The highway is a two-lane road that runs along Bayou Lafourche and through many small communities. It floods during storms and often becomes impassable due to weather or accidents.

Assistant Port Director Davie Breaux notes that delays on Highway 1 due to an accident and lasting several hours are not unusual. And Breaux says that although the port is on relatively high ground and does not have a significant problem with flooding, the roughly 15-mile section of road north of the port floods frequently and the debris left behind will hamper transportation to the port for several days (Breaux, personal interview, 1999).

The highway is of vital importance to the local community as well as the offshore industry. Many of the necessary supplies for the industry are brought in by truck to the port. According to Executive Director Ted Falgout, on an average day approximately one thousand trucks come in and out of the port. No other land transportation is available and there is no railroad. A five-acre truck stop, pictured in Figure 7, was recently built. The increased truck traffic due to the growth of offshore activity is significantly affecting the highway's condition. Current and future growth in OCS development is expected to increase the need to upgrade the road (see the appendix).

Another problem presented by the poor highway is the speed and effectiveness of a response to an environmental disaster such as an oil spill in the Gulf of Mexico. This could threaten many environmentally sensitive areas such as Louisiana's highly productive estuaries. Further, Highway 1 is the only avenue for hurricane evacuation. In addition to thousands of OCS workers and much valuable industrial equipment, the towns of Grand Isle and Leeville as well as Port Fourchon are dependent on this single evacuation route.

Figure 4. Large vessels requiring a deeper draft can be accommodated at Port Fourchon. The increased activity in deepwater oil and gas activities has made the port vitally important to industry.

Figure 5. Deepwater supply vessel is serviced at C-Port facility, Port Fourchon, Louisiana. Covered docks allow for the loading and unloading of vessels in all weather; one stop for loading water, fuel, and drilling materials onto supply vessels is faster and more cost-effective than conventional port facilities.

Figure 6. Additional C-Port docking facilities are currently under construction at Port Fourchon, Louisiana.

Figure 7. Because of the enormous amount of commercial traffic to the
port, a large truck stop is being built.

Strain on the local infrastructure is also evident in the availability of freshwater; oil and gas companies must bring in water daily by barge. The industry requires a great deal of potable water and meeting the needs of the local community in addition to industry needs has created a problem. These local concerns were reflected recently in headlines appearing in one of the state's major daily newspapers. "Grand Isle confident it has plenty of water for holiday weekend," proclaimed The Times-Picayune (May 29, 1999) in anticipation of Memorial Day (Barbier, 1999).

According to a recent final environmental impact statement dealing with oil and gas lease sales in the Gulf of Mexico, "Needs specific to these deepwater projects may result in more focused stresses placed on areas that are capable of supporting these large-scale development projects (e.g., ports that can handle deepwater draft service vessels)." These stresses include those placed on the local water supply and Highway 1 due to activity associated with Port Fourchon. The publication notes, in particular, that Highway 1 will likely deteriorate as a result of increased oil and gas activity (U.S. Department of the Interior, Minerals Management Service, 1997).

A shortage of labor in the local community is yet another problem for business and industry. For example, Edison Chouest recently located a shipyard in north Louisiana in order to find enough workers to staff the facility. However, the offshore industry operates with work schedules that allow for it to draw workers from a geographical area well beyond the local community, the parish, or even the state. Working one week, two weeks, or one month "on" followed by an equal amount of time "off" means workers can live far from the rigs in the Gulf and its land base. The number of out-of-state workers employed in the offshore oil industry is evident in the parking lots at Port Fourchon. Figure 8 shows examples of vehicles with licenses from out of the state. A check of license plates (June 2, 1999) at one parking lot at the ERA Aviation helicopter facility revealed that 54% of the vehicles were registered in other states, some as far away as Arizona and Alaska. More than one in four vehicles were registered in

Figure 8. The offshore industry employs many out of state
workers. Parking lots at Port Fourchon typically have
large numbers of out of state vehicles reflecting both the
need for labor and the economic importance of the port
far beyond the local community and Louisiana.

13

Mississippi. Sixteen percent were registered in Texas. Similar checks at three other parking lot facilities at the port in late June 1999 also attest to the large numbers of out of state workers employed in the industry (see Table 5).

Port Commission Surveys Offshore Workers

Informal information on the influx of out of state workers abounds, but not many attempts to quantify this information have been undertaken in a systematic fashion. However, the Greater Lafourche Port Commission recently conducted a survey of hundreds of workers at the port with the cooperation of three helicopter transport companies. These companies are involved in the business of ferrying workers from Port Fourchon to offshore facilities. This presented an ideal opportunity to survey offshore workers with a brief questionnaire. In addition, a pretest of the survey administered to a small number of offshore workers revealed a high level of interest on the part of those questioned. A majority of those answering the pretest took the time to add written comments expressing their views in more detail although written comments were not formally solicited.

The port commission distributed 300 surveys in June 1999; 200 surveys were completed and returned. Of the 200 respondents, only 23 (11.5%) live in Lafourche Parish. Of the remaining group, 93 (46.5%) live in state and 84 (42%) live out of state. Ninety-seven workers (48.5%) reported that they travel to the port on a biweekly schedule; 49 workers (24.5%) come to work on a monthly schedule. Thirty-two respondents (16%) indicated that they travel to the port on a weekly basis; 14 workers (7%) commute daily to the port: and the remaining group of 8 respondents (4%) come to the port on another schedule. The survey results reveal a substantial out-of-state workforce and are consistent with counts of car license plates in several parking lots at the port.

The port commission survey also asked those surveyed to rate the quality and safety of Louisiana Highway 1. Everyone responding to the survey indicated that they traveled on the highway. The average rating or score given the road was 2.52, based on a scale of 1 to 10 with 10 being the highest possible rating and 1 the lowest. The survey did not inquire about other heavily traveled roads in the parish such as Louisiana Highway 308, but other information indicates that these other roads also are not highly regarded by workers traveling in and through the parish (see Table 6).

The port commission also inquired about the number of people who work in Federal waters. Of the 200 workers surveyed, 170 or 85% indicated that they worked in Federal waters offshore. Of this group, only 14 or 8.2% live in Lafourche Parish; another 84 or 49.4% live in the Louisiana, but not in the parish, and 72 workers or 42.4% indicated that they live out of state. The results for this group of respondents working in Federal waters are similar to the overall survey. The findings indicated a majority of the workers travel to the port on a biweekly or monthly schedule and the rating given Highway 1 was low, 2.48 (see Table 7).

Local Services Under Strain

Out-of-state workers sometimes become new residents, they can present the local community with added stress on infrastructure and services. Local government is experiencing higher revenues to offset some of the increases in expenditures to provide services, but the amount of new revenue is exceeded by the new costs associated with increased oil and gas

Table 5: Vehicle License Plates by State, Selected Parking Lots at Port Fourchon
June 1999

Lot and Date Sampled	Total No.*	LA*	Out of State*	MS	TX	AL	FL	AR	GA	AK	AZ	TN	MO	OK	VA	IL	CO	NC
ERA Aviation 6/2/99	186 (100%)	86 (46%)	100 (54%)	48	29	7	7	2	2	1	1	1	1	1	0	0	0	0
Martin Terminal** 6/25/99	145 (100%)	79 (55.5%)	66 (45.5%)	24	22	9	6	1	0	0	0	0	1	1	1	1	0	0
Air Logistics 6/25/99	145 (100%)	69 (48%)	76 (52%)	31	23	5	8	2	2	0	0	1	0	3	0	0	1	0
Petroleum Helicopters Inc.*** 6/25/99	411 (100%)	242 (59%)	169 (41%)	87	30	24	17	4	0	0	0	1	3	1	1	0	0	1

* Percentage of total in parentheses.

** Includes two parking lots.

*** Includes three parking lots.

15

Table 6: Greater Lafourche Port Commission Survey
(Summer 1999)

Totals and Averages Based on 200 Surveys

Do you travel on Louisiana Highway 1? Yes = 200 (100%)
                                        No = 0   (0%)

Please give us your opinion of the highway. Average = 2.52 from 200 questionnaires
Please rate the overall quality and safety of
Highway 1 on a scale of 1 to 10. A score of 10
is the best possible score and a score of one is
the lowest score.

Do you work in the oil industry or business Yes = 200 (100%)
associated with the oil industry?   No = 0   (0%)

   If yes, do you work in Federal waters Yes = 170 (85%)
   (more than three miles out in the Gulf?) No = 30   (15%)

Do you live in Lafourche Parish? Yes = 23   (11.5%)
                                  No = 177 (88.5%)

   If no, do you live in Louisiana? Yes = 93 (46.5%)
                                     No = 84 (42%)

    Note: Total Living in Louisiana = 116 (58%)
         Total Out of State   = 84 (42%)
         Of the 116 Living in Louisiana, 23 live in Lafourche Parish

How often do you travel to Port Fourchon? Daily   = 14 (7%)
                                           Weekly   = 32 (16%)
                                           Biweekly   = 97 (48.5%)
                                           Monthly   = 49 (24.5%)
                                           Other   = _8_ (4%)
                                                        200

Source: Greater Lafourche Port Commission (July 1999).

Table 7: Survey Results for Those Working in Federal Waters
(Summer 1999)

Out of 200 surveys 170 responded yes to working in Federal waters
(more than three miles out in the Gulf).
These are their responses.

Do you travel on Louisiana Highway 1?	Yes = 170	(100%)
	No = 0	(0%)

Please give us your opinion of the highway.   Average = 2.48 from 170 questionnaires
Please rate the overall quality and safety of
Highway 1 on a scale of 1 to 10. A score of 10
is the best possible score and a score of one is
the lowest score.

Do you work in the oil industry or business associated with the oil industry?	Yes = 170	(100%)
	No = 0	(0%)
Do you live in Lafourche Parish?	Yes = 14	(8%)
	No = 156	(92%)
If no, do you live in Louisiana?	Yes = 84	(49%)
	No = 72	(42%)

Note: Total Living in Louisiana = 98 (58%)
          Total Living Out of State = 72 (42%)
          Of the 98 Living in Louisiana, 14 live in Lafourche Parish

How often do you travel to Port Fourchon?	Daily	= 6 (3.5%)
	Weekly	= 30 (18%)
	Biweekly	= 79 (46.5%)
	Monthly	= 48 (28%)
	Other	= _7 (4%)
		170

Source: Greater Lafourche Port Commission (July 1999).

activity on the Outer Continental Shelf. This is true chiefly for two reasons. First, many of the increased costs to local government are difficult to quantify or, at least to date, have not been estimated. Second, some locally provided services are tied to the unique needs of the oil and gas offshore industry. For example, schools, city water, law enforcement, and roads have been particularly affected by the growth of offshore development.

Schools and other local agencies are being called upon to do more. The local school system is incurring additional costs due to larger populations stemming from increased OCS activity. Further, the in-migration of foreign workers has placed demands on community services beyond those expected with a growing population. For example, the local school system is now facing the issues and challenges related to bilingual education as Spanish speakers begin to move to the area. This is often a difficult task for large metropolitan school systems, and the local community in this case is rather small and strongly French in its background and history.

Older people in this part of the state relate that they grew up speaking French; they were first exposed to English when they started school. One retired tugboat operator recalls that as a child he spoke French at home, but when he started school the situation changed. In addition to being taught in English, children were prohibited from speaking French anywhere at school. If someone was caught, "You had to write 500 times 'I will not speak French on the school ground'" (Coen, 1999). Integrating Spanish speakers into the local community has been challenging according to many local residents.

Residential development in Lafourche Parish has increased in recent years placing more demands on local services. The number of residential units increased at a rate of 14% annually between 1988 and 1997. The level of construction has been particularly strong since 1995.

Local law enforcement agencies are also experiencing additional demands on services and resources due to the increased level of OCS activity in recent years. Lafourche Parish Sheriff Craig Webre has three principal concerns with respect to law enforcement: transients, traffic, and victimization. The number of transients in the parish makes enforcement and apprehension more difficult, because criminals are harder to identify in the transient population. There has also been an upswing in vice crime in the parish, which the sheriff attributes to the influx of transient laborers. Transients lack the community ties and civic pride that help maintain law and order in the community.

According to Sheriff Webre, the parish has experienced both increased traffic congestion as well as more accidents and fatalities as a result of the higher level of offshore development in recent years. The unique geography of the parish, which is nearly 100 miles long and is divided by Bayou Lafourche, combined with the lack of a good secondary road system have created difficulties. Local residents must contend daily with commercial traffic to and from the port as well as commuting offshore workers. The two main state highways, Highway 1 and Highway 308, run roughly from north to south on either side of Bayou Lafourche. According to the sheriff, the stretches of these roads between Highway 90 and Port Fourchon are particularly busy due to OCS development. In response to increased complaints in the last three years the sheriff's office has concentrated additional highway enforcement efforts through grant money to three areas near the port: Leeville, Louisiana Highway 24 between Bourg and Larose, and Highway 308 in Larose. Because local roads such as Highway 308 were never designed for high speeds and heavy traffic, driving conditions can be hazardous. For example, Highway 308 has virtually no shoulder and many curves. There is no room for driver error, according to the sheriff.

The sheriff is also concerned that the influx of foreigners means law enforcement personnel must deal with people who have significant language and cultural barriers. In addition,

18

the sheriff worries that many foreign residents do not possess the resources or the knowledge to report crimes and thus are easy victims for criminals. In sum, Sheriff Webre maintains that the economic activity generated by OCS development has brought many economic benefits to the area, but it is important to understand that there are also hidden costs such as the need for additional services (Webre, personal interview, 1999).

A recent study conducted by three sociologists at the University of New Orleans underscores many of the same local law enforcement concerns. Seydlitz, et al., (1999) report an association between oil and gas development, particularly rapid development, and increased lethal violence (homicide and suicide). The researchers examined nearly four decades of data for more than 20 Louisiana parishes and compared the rates of violence with Southern states as well as the nation as a whole. They theorize that rapid urbanization and immigration create population heterogeneity and reduce the informal social control placed on the individual. These changes contribute to social problems.

The mayor of Lockport, J. B. Townsend, Jr., echoes many of the same concerns. Although Lockport is approximately 50 miles from the port, the town has been affected by offshore development. The municipality of Lockport is only one square mile with a population of 3000; within a 4-mile radius of the town, there are 15,000 residents. Three major shipyards operate in the area building primarily, though not exclusively, for the needs of the oil and gas industry. The economy of the area has been good in recent years, according to the mayor. The demand for labor is high and the revenues of the town have been rising. Social demands on the community have also increased. The town recently added another deputy to its small force in response to increased crime. The mayor believes that the influx of transient labor has led to more barroom brawls, loitering, and theft, according to the mayor.

Increased traffic has become a problem for local residents; many complaints involved the difficulty encountered by locals attempting to cross Louisiana Highway 1, which runs through the center of town. The mayor notes seeing with great regularity cars with out-of-state license plates and truck traffic related to the oil and gas industry passing through Lockport. The condition of roads in Lockport has been affected and the town recently completed street improvements.

There are other ways Lockport has been affected by offshore development. Entire families from other states have come to town with the adult family members looking for work. Finding work is not usually a problem but finding housing can be very difficult. A housing shortage has been a major problem, according to Mayor Townsend. The area has only about 100 rental units, although approximately another 100 units are presently under construction.

Churches have helped newcomers as have individual citizens. The mayor remembers one mother with two children who came to Lockport with a transient worker. After he disappeared, the family relied on locals for help. Someone gave them a place to live temporarily and the children enrolled in school, but the mother was not capable of supporting herself and her children. Eventually, the family returned to their home out of state. These are not usually the kinds of social problems faced in small rural communities (Townsend, personal interview, 1999).

Dirk Barrios, general manager of the Lafourche Parish Water District No. 1, is very familiar with the demands of a growing offshore industry. According to Barrios, increased activity and new developments in drilling technology have led to greater demands for potable water by the industry. It is necessary for some of the water supply to be transported on barges to large customers, because the existing capacity of the pipelines is insufficient. In June 1999, the offshore industry consumed 16% of the total output for the entire parish. According to Barrios, the demand for water has been stable or rising for several years.

The needs of the oil industry have determined the direction and scope of improvements being made in the parish's only water district. A few years ago the water district sold bonds to fund $10 million in improvements to the system, primarily directed at providing more water to Port Fourchon. The district, which encompasses Lafourche Parish, has two stations. The larger facility, with a current capacity of 8 million gallons, will be increased by 50% to a capacity of 12 million gallons. Most of the additional water will be directed to the southern part of the parish where the port is located. The project is in progress and Barrios is somewhat doubtful that the available money will entirely cover the cost of the completed project. It is difficult for a rural water district with smaller resources to meet all the demands of a global the industry, according to Barrios (Barrios, personal interview, 1999).

Conclusion

Recent developments in offshore deepwater oil and gas exploration and development in the Gulf of Mexico have brought new economic growth to Port Fourchon and the surrounding community. Increased economic activity associated with providing onshore support for the oil and gas industry has provided economic benefits to the area. However, the demands of this new growth has meant new challenges for the port and the local community. Strains on the infrastructure are evidenced by the condition of the roads and the volume of traffic, and the water system's current expansion. Stress on local public agencies has been noted by local officials at the municipal and parish (or county) levels.

References

Barbier, S. "Grand Isle confident it has plenty of water for holiday weekend." The Times-Picayune, May 29, 1999, sec. B, page 1.

Barrios, D. R., 1999, Personal interview. General Manager, Lafourche Parish Water District No. 1, Lockport, Louisiana.

Breaux, D., 1999, Personal interview. Port Fourchon Assistant Director, Fourchon, Louisiana.

Coen, C., 1999, "Pirogue Preservation," The Sunday Advocate Magazine, August 1, p. 18-19.

Cranswick, D. and J. Regg, 1997, Deepwater in the Gulf of Mexico: America's New Frontier, U.S. Department of the Interior, Minerals Management Service, Gulf of Mexico OCS Region, OCS Report MMS 97-0004, New Orleans, 43 p.

Falgout, T., Executive Director of Port Fourchon, Galliano, Louisiana. Personal interview. May 21, 1999.

Greater Lafourche Port Commission, 1999, Daily Average Number and Total Number of Vessels by Type from January 1998 to December 1998.

Greater Lafourche Port Commission, 1999, Daily Average Number and Total Number of Vessels by Type from January 1999 to May 1999.

Greater Lafourche Port Commission, 1999, Greater Lafourche Port Survey.

Greater Lafourche Port Commission, 1999, Leases, Acreage, and Waterfront Growth from 1990 to 1998.

Griggs, T., 1999, "Layoffs ripple through economy", The Advocate, June 26, p. 1A-4A.

Langley, C., J. Regg, D. Marin, J. M. Melancon, and M. Prendergast, 1998, "Deepwater in the Gulf of Mexico: An Update of America's New Frontier," U.S. Department of the Interior, Minerals Management Service, Gulf of Mexico OCS Regional Office. OCS Report MMS 98-0003.

Melancon, J. M., and D. S. Roby, 1998, Gulf of Mexico Outer Continental Shelf Daily Oil and Gas Production Rate Projection from 1998 through 2002, U.S. Department of the Interior, Minerals Management Service, Gulf of Mexico OCS Region, OCS Report MMS 98-0013, New Orleans, 16 p.

Melancon, J. M., and R. D. Baud, 1999, Gulf of Mexico Outer Continental Shelf Daily Oil and Gas Production Rate Projections from 1999 through 2003, Minerals Management Service, Gulf of Mexico OCS Regional Office, OCS Report MMS 99-0016, New Orleans, 20 p.

Seydlitz, R., P. Jenkins, and V. Gunter, 1999, "Impact of petroleum development on lethal violence", Impact Assessment Project Appraisal, Vol. 17, No. 2, p. 115-131.

Townsend, J. B., Jr., 1999, Personal interview. Mayor of Lockport, Louisiana.

Turk, L., 1999, "Oil and gas stages comeback", The Greater Baton Rouge Business Report, July 6-July 19, p. 45, 57-58.

U.S. Department of the Army, Corps of Engineers, New Orleans District, 1994. Port Fourchon, Louisiana, Feasibility Report and Environmental Impact Statement, Plate 1, August 1994.

U.S. Department of the Interior, Minerals Management Service, 1997, Gulf of Mexico OCS Oil and Gas Lease Sales 169, 172, 175, 178, and 182: Central Planning Area Final Environmental Impact Statement, OCS EIS/EA MMS 97-0033.

Webre, C., 1999, Personal interview. Lafourche Parish Sheriff, Thibodaux, Louisiana.

White, R., 1999, Personal interview. Director of Business Development, Edison Chouest, Galliano, Louisiana.

APPENDIX

AN ANALYSIS OF LOUISIANA HIGHWAY 1
IN RELATION TO EXPANDING OIL AND GAS ACTIVITIES
IN THE CENTRAL GULF OF MEXICO

Jimine Guo, Ph.D., David Hughes, Ph.D., and Walter R. Keithly, Ph.D.,
Louisiana State University, Baton Rouge, LA

Under Contract with Minerals Management Service,
U.S. Department of Interior

March 1998

Table Of Contents

I. INTRODUCTION

The U.S. domestic production of oil equaled almost 2.4 billion barrels in 1995 while production of gas equaled 18, 902 billion cubic feet. Production of oil from the Gulf of Mexico Outer Continental Shelf (OCS)[1] in 1995 (357 million barrels) represented 15% of the nation's 2.4 billion barrels produced while production of gas from the Gulf of Mexico OCS (5,015 billion cubic feet) represented more than a quarter of the nation's total domestic supply.

Heretofore, the vast majority of oil-and-gas production from the Gulf of Mexico OCS has been shallow-water based (defined as taken from depths of less than 1,000 feet). Because most of the conventional fields were mature and moving towards production decline, the Gulf of Mexico was being referred to as the "Dead Sea" as recently as the late 1980's. This characterization has been reversed during the 1990's, however, as a result of several factors. These factors include, but are not limited to: (a) favorable economic conditions, (b) recent discoveries in the deepwater shelf, (c) deepwater royalty relief, and (d) the use of new and improved technology which has permitted the extension of the conventional fields and increased discoveries on fields in deeper waters (Cranswick and Regg, 1997). Particularly pronounced growth since the early 1990's has been in association with deepwater activities (in excess of 1,000 feet) and there is cautious optimism that these offshore activities will continue, and likely expand, well into the next century.

The rejuvenation of oil-and-gas activities in the Gulf of Mexico OCS and the rapid movement of these activities to the deepwater fields have raised the issue as to whether the current infrastructure is sufficient to adequately handle the anticipated increase in service demands placed thereon. This is particularly relevant in light of the fact that only a few ports in the area (e.g., Port Fourchon, Gulfport, Mobile, and Galveston) are equipped to service the needs associated with the deepwater development in the Central Gulf of Mexico; i.e., the region where the majority of future activities are expected.

One component of infrastructure of particular concern relates to the ability of the current road system to adequately handle the increased traffic expected to be forthcoming with the increased offshore activities. This ability entails two dimensions: (a) a traffic congestion dimension and (2) a road deterioration dimension. The congestion dimension reflects a need to transport an increasing number of workers and equipment in relation to increasing activities. The deterioration dimension reflects the increased "wear and tear" on the existing road system generally associated with the increased truck traffic that will be required to transport the equipment and other factors of production needed for the development and construction of new deepwater wells as well as for the routine maintenance/service of existing and as yet developed wells.

---

[1] The Outer Continental Shelf (OCS), with some exceptions, refers to the area of oceans beyond state boundaries out to 200 miles offshore.

The overall purpose of this report to examine the ability of LA Highway 1[2] to adequately support the increased services that will be required in association with enhanced deepwater oil-and-gas activities in the Central Gulf of Mexico. Highway 1 traverses approximately ninety miles in distance and extends from north Lafourche Parish to Grand Isle, an inhabited barrier island along coast (see Figure 1 below).

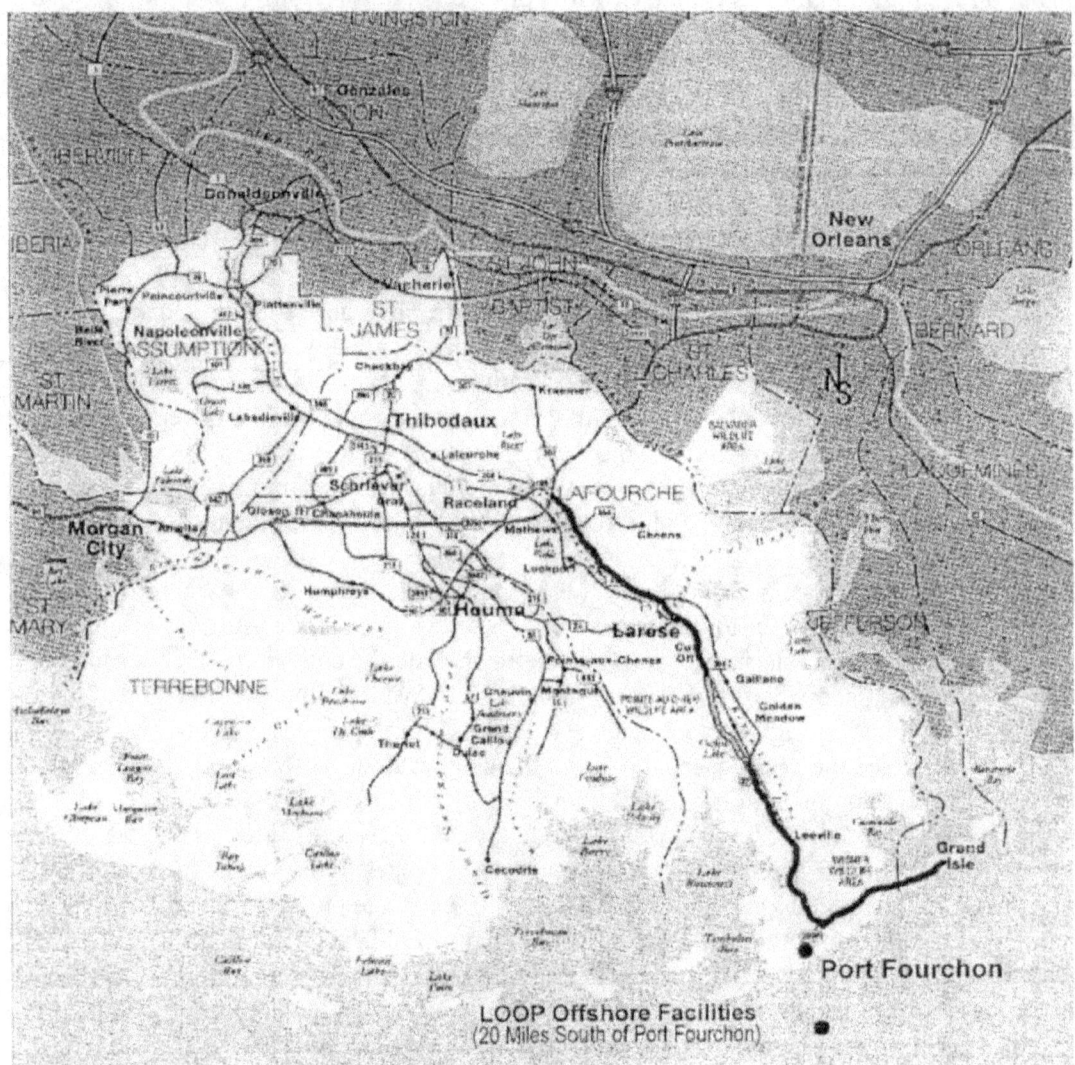

Figure 1: Map of Highway 1 through southern Louisiana

It is the primary north-south corridor through Lafourche Parish and is the primary transportation route for trucks entering and exiting Port Fourchon, a primary service-support port for deepwater oil-and-gas activities in the Central Gulf. Highway 1 is largely a rural, two- lane arterial road which passes through many of the principal cities and towns in Lafourche Parish. The road, as discussed in more detail later in the report,

_____

[2]   LA Highway 1 is referred to throughout the report as LA 1.

2

varies in quality depending upon section and is considered by many to be inadequate to handle current, much less anticipated future, traffic. As such, the LA 1 Coalition was recently formed to garner support for road enhancement.

The report, in order to achieve the overall purpose discussed above, proceeds as follows. First, a brief review of historical oil-and-gas activities in the Gulf of Mexico is provided along with a discussion of future prospects. Then, a brief overview of Port Fourchon is given. Third, an analysis of congestion and deterioration dimensions of LA 1 under current and anticipated future growth scenerios (associated with expansion of Central Gulf of Mexico oil-and gas activities) is provided. Some brief concluding remarks and recommendations are presented in the final section of the report.

II. GULF OF MEXICO OCS OIL- AND- GAS PRODUCTION AND ACTIVITIES

To assess oil-and-gas activities in the Gulf of Mexico, historical trends are first presented. Then, attention is turned to analysis of future activities based on available forecasts and other relevant information.

A. Historical and Current Activities

A.1. Oil Production

Production of oil from the Gulf of Mexico (OCS) for the 1985-96 period is illustrated in Figure 2. Overall, annual production ranged from a low of 275 million barrels in 1990 to a high of 366 million barrels in 1996 and averaged 320 million barrels for the 12-year period of analysis.

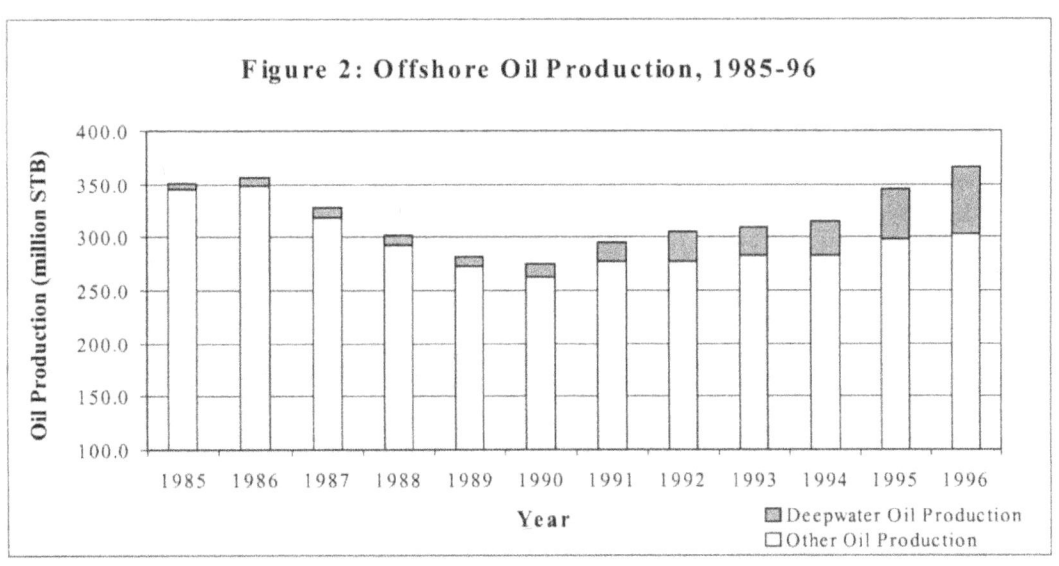

Examination of the data suggests two distinct trends during the 12-year period. The first trend, from 1985 to 1990, is one of a sharp decline in total production. Overall, total

3

production during this period fell by about 20%. The second trend, evident from 1990 through 1996, is one of increasing total production. During this period, production of oil from the Gulf of Mexico (OCS) advanced by more than 30% with the last three years exhibiting particularly pronounced production increases.

The increase in production since 1990 is, by and large, the result of expanding deepwater activities (defined as production from more than 1,000 feet). Specifically, deepwater production of oil from the Gulf of Mexico equaled 12 million barrels in 1990. By 1996, deepwater production had advanced more than five-fold to 63 million barrels see Figure 2). Overall, the share of Gulf of Mexico OCS oil production represented by deepwater activities equaled 17% in 1996 compared to only about four percent in 1990.

A.2. Gas Production

Natural gas production from the Gulf of Mexico (OCS) is given in Figure 3 for the 1985-96 period. Total production, as indicated, advanced from 4.1×10^9 mcf in 1985 to 5.0×10^9 mcf in 1996, approximately one quarter. Production of natural gas from deepwater activities advanced from 3.1×10^7 mcf in 1990 to 3.0×10^8 mcf in 1996, almost ten fold. Overall, the share of Gulf of Mexico OCS production derived from deepwater activities advanced from less than one percent in 1990 to about six percent in 1996.

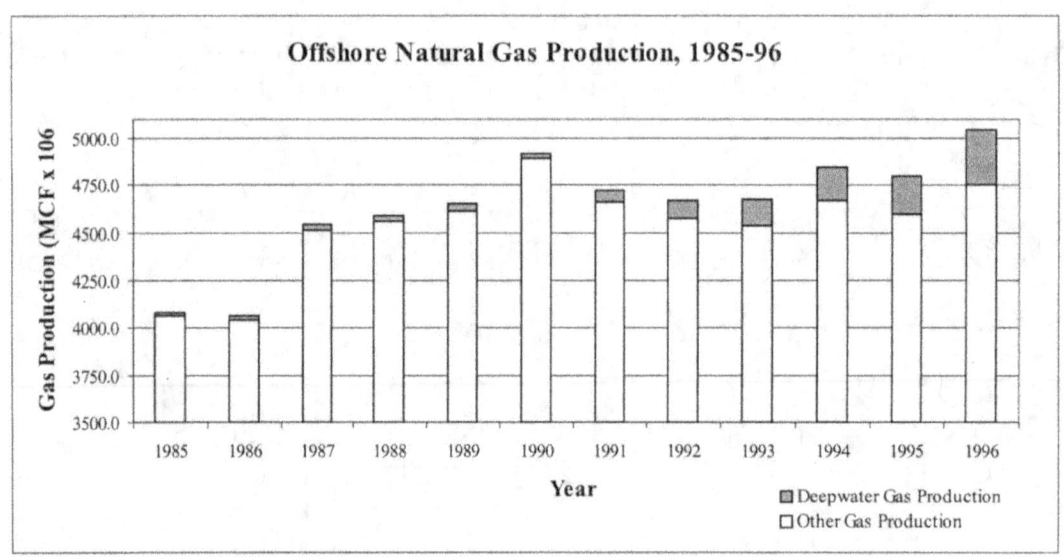

Figure 3: Gulf of Mexico Offshore Natural Gas Production, 1985-96

B. Future Activities

Predicting future Gulf of Mexico oil-and-gas activities is, at best, imprecise with the level of imprecision increasing in relation to the length of forecast period.[3] Having given this cautionary note, some forecasts and indications of future activities are contained herein.

Analysis conducted by Melancon et al. (1997) indicates that oil production from the Gulf of Mexico will increase in the range of 50% to 75% between 1996 and 2000, or at a rate of 10% to 15% per year (see Table 1 below). Depending on assumptions used in the analysis, production of gas will either rise by as much as 25% or decline by almost 15%. Furthermore, Melancon et al. suggest that production from deepwater fields will account for 56%-65% of the total Gulf of Mexico oil production by the year 2000 (compared to the 17% as of 1996) and from 19% to 28% of the total Gulf of Mexico gas supply (compared to the six percent as of 1996).

Table 1: Daily Oil and Gas Production Rate Projections - GOM					
	1996	1997	1998	1999	2000
Low Oil MBOPD* (Decline Used)	1,097	1,230	1,240	1,545	1,660
High Oil MBOPD* (No Decline used)	1,097	1,300	1,407	1,730	1,932
Low Gas Bcfd** (Decline Used)	13.82	13.32	13.56	13.07	12.02
High Gas Bcfd** (No Decline Used)	13.82	15.80	16.00	16.70	17.20
* Oil in MBOPD includes condensate. ** Gas in BCFPD includes associated or casinghead gas					

The oil production forecasts cited by Melancon et al. (1997) compare favorably with those recently published in the *Petroleum Economist* (1997). Specifically, forecasts reported in the report suggest that Federal offshore oil production from the Gulf of Mexico will advance from 1,328 thousand barrels per day in 1997 to about 1,900 thousand barrels per day by the year 2000, an increase of more than 40% (Table 2 on following two pages). Production from the Central Gulf of Mexico during the period is expected to advance from about 70% of the total in 1997 to more than 80% of the total by the year 2000.

---

[3] In one recent economic study, for example, Walls (1994) predicted that Gulf of Mexico oil production would decline from about 277 million barrels in 1989 to about 160 million barrels by the year 2000. Similarly, production of gas was predicted to fall from 4275 bcf to 3160 bcf. Walls results appear to under-predict for at least two reasons. First, the prices (oil and gas wellhead prices) used in the forecasting exercise are well below the prices currently being received. Second, the author, understandably, failed to forsee the expansion in deepwater activities.

Table2: Offshore Oil Production in the Gulf of Mexico

	Water Depth	Production (Thousand b/d)						
		1994	1995	1996	1997	1998	1999	2000
Federal offshore central Gulf		782.0	830.3	927.7	1093.0	1205.0	1354.0	1545.0
Oil fields								
- crude		644.0	625.8	607.9	576.0	487.0	433.0	420.0
- condensates		118.9	132.5	183.8	185.0	190.0	195.0	206.0
Viosca Knoll								
Tahoe	1,500	1.0	2.0	5.0	8.0	10.0	10.0	10.0
Pompano A	1,800	---	23.0	30.0	35.0	40.0	40.0	45.0
Pompano B	1,930	---	---	5.0	10.0	20.0	30.0	30.0
Neptune	1,930	---	---	---	15.0	25.0	25.0	25.0
Ram-Powell	3,218	---	---	---	30.0	45.0	50.0	80.0
Petronius	1,750	---	---	---	---	---	50.0	60.0
Mississippi Canyon								
Mars	2,940	---	---	33.0	130.0	145.0	150.0	150.0
Ursa	3,950	---	---	---	---	45.0	75.0	145.0
Gemini	3,393	---	---	---	---	10.0	30.0	50.0
Mickey	4,350	---	---	---	---	---	---	15.0

Table2: Offshore Oil Production in the Gulf of Mexico (Continued)

	Water Depth	Production (Thousand b/d)						
		1994	1995	1996	1997	1998	1999	2000
Green Canyon								
Jolliet	1,760	8.0	8.0	7.0	5.0	4.0	2.0	---
Popeye	2,000	---	1.0	1.0	1.0	1.0	1.0	1.0
Troika	2,761	---	---	---	---	20.0	40.0	55.0
Olivella	---	---	---	---	---	---	---	20.0
Genesis	2,597	---	---	---	---	25.0	50.0	60.0
Allegheny	3,225	---	---	---	---	---	10.0	20.0
Fuji	4,243	---	---	---	---	---	---	---
Ship Shoal								
Mahogany	---	---	---	5.0	22.0	30.0	30.0	35.0
Agate	---	---	---	---	---	10.0	15.0	15.0
Alexandrite	---	---	---	---	---	---	---	5.0
Ewing Bank								
Block 873	---	10.0	20.0	30.0	40.0	40.0	30.0	25.0
Sunday Silence	---	---	---	---	---	10.0	15.0	15.0
Morpeth	---	---	---	---	---	---	25.0	30.0
Federal offshore western Gulf		81.4	112.9	151.5	235.0	292.0	311.0	352.0

Source: IEA - *Global Offshore Oil Prospects to 2000*, with additional information from *Petroleum Economist*

The Mississippi Canyon, with anticipated production of 360 thousand barrels per day by the year 2000, will account for just less than a quarter of the total 1,545 barrels per day produced from Federal waters in the Central Gulf of Mexico. The Viasoca Knoll and the Green Canyon will account for another 16% and 10% of the Central Gulf of Mexico production, respectively. These fields, all easily accessible from Port Fourchon, are all deepwater as indicated by the information contained in Table 2.

While the aforementioned studies provide the most direct evidence of expanding deepwater activities in the Gulf of Mexico, tangential evidence is also substantial. For example, lease sales in the Central Planning Area advanced from 139 in 1992 to 157 in 1996. The number of deepwater leases awarded, furthermore, increased from 24 in 1992 to 69 in 1994 and then almost quadrupled to 274 in 1995 and increased again to 822 in 1996. Overall, the number of deepwater tracts leased as a percentage of total tracts leased equaled 55% in 1996 compared to only 12% in 1992.

Other indicators of deepwater activity potential include: (a) applications for permit to drill approved by the MMS, (b) the monthly average of rigs drilling, (c) production stage, and (4) reserves stage. Overall, the number of applications for permits to drill in deepwaters of the Gulf of Mexico which were approved by the MMS increased from 39 in 1992 to 126 in 1996. The average monthly number of rigs in drilling stage, during the same period of time, advanced from three to 19 while the number of fields in production increased from six to 16 (as of June). Finally, the total number of deepwater fields with proven reserves increased from 15 in 1992 to 25 as of June 1996. Proven reserves of oil in these deepwater fields as of June 1996 equaled 1,370 mmbls while proven gas reserves equaled 4.92 tcf.

While past activities do not necessarily reflect future activities, the information provided in the previous few paragraphs does suggest significant future activities in the deepwaters of the Central Gulf of Mexico, *ceteris paribus*. In the absence of a sharp price decline, there appears no reason to believe that deepwater activities will falter in the near future. In fact, given the increasing lease sales etc. a strong argument can be made that activities will likely increase by a "substantial" amount.

III. PORT FOURCHON

Port Fourchon is situated at the mouth of Bayou Lafourche. It is Louisiana's only port on the Gulf of Mexico. While catering to several business sectors, the primary purpose of the port is to support offshore oil-and-gas activities throughout the Central Gulf of Mexico. At present, more than 600 offshore platforms are located within a 40-mile radius of Port Fourchon and, according to a recently completed study by the Corps of Engineers, Port Fourchon will be within the service area of almost 60% of all offshore drilling activities anticipated to occur off the Louisiana coast over the next thirty years. In addition, a substantial number of the deepwater prospects are within the Port Fourchon service area (see Figure 4 on following page).

8

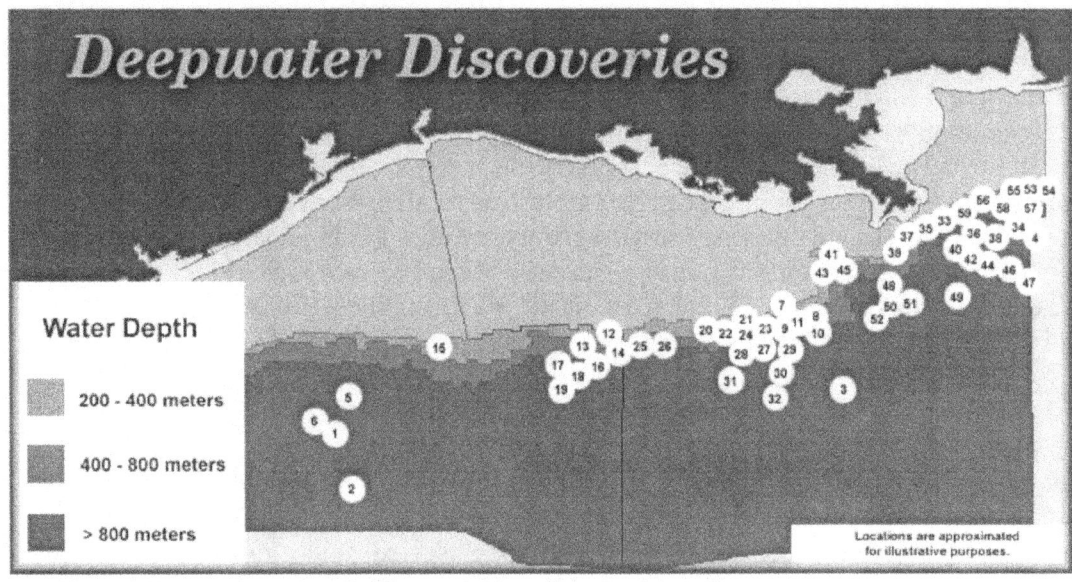

Figure 4: Present Deepwater Drilling Activities off the Louisiana Coast

IV. CAPACITY AND DETERIORATION CONDITIONS ALONG LA 1

There exists considerable concern, as noted in the Introduction, as to whether LA 1 can adequately handle the increased traffic expected to be forthcoming in relation to expanding offshore oil-and-gas activities in the Central Gulf of Mexico; particularly the deepwater activities. Two points of concern, as mentioned, relate to congestion (i.e., capacity) and deterioration. A quantitative as well as qualitative evaluation of these two concerns is presented below.

A. Highway Traffic Capacity Analysis for Port Fourchon

In the analysis for the economy of proposed highway facilities, the performance of motor vehicles on the highway is an important factor. The two elements of major importance are the speed of traffic and the volume of the traffic, which are interrelated. The primary traffic flow elements include flow, density and speed. Traffic capacity is the maximum (hourly) flow rate at which vehicles can reasonably be expected to traverse a point or uniform section of a lane or roadway during a given time period under prevailing roadway, traffic, and control condition. The traffic flows reasonably well when the flow rate is less than optimum (capacity), but excessive delay and congestion occur when the flow rate is at or near capacity. Capacity analysis therefore involves the quantitative evaluation of the capability of a road section to carry traffic. When the demand volume increases vehicle interaction and density increases, resulting in the gradual lowing of the speed than can be safely achieved by drivers. So, for a given capacity, the level of operating performance, the quality of flow, changes with the traffic density on the highway.

9

The level of operating performance is indicated by the concept of level of service (LOS), which uses qualitative measures that characterize both operational conditions within a traffic stream and motorists' and passengers' perception. The determination of traffic capacity involves utilizing mathematical relationships among the elements of that affect traffic flow. The primary objective of this analysis is to provide the potential changes in the highway operating performance for the two-lane rural highways, which lead to Port Fourchon. The change of level of service mainly involves the anticipated rapid growth of traffic demand (truck flows) in that area, because of the expected high growth rate of the local economy. This expected high growth rate is a function of rejuvenated oil-and-gas activities in the Central Gulf of Mexico.

A.1 Basic Concept and Relationships in Traffic Capacity Analysis

For purpose of analysis, four concepts relating to traffic capacity are utilized in the current study. The theoretical foundations associated with these four concepts are presented below. Then, the empirical findings are presented.

A.1.1 The definition of level of service (LOS)

As previously indicated, the level of operating performance is characterized by the concept of "Level of Service" (LOS). LOS quantitatively measures both the operating conditions within a traffic system and how these conditions are perceived by drivers and passengers. It is related to the physical characteristics of the highway and the different operating characteristics that can occur when the highway carries different traffic volumes. Although speed-flow-density relationships are the principal factor affecting the level of service of a highway segment under ideal conditions, factors such as lane width, lateral observation, traffic composition, grade, driver population, and speed also affect the maximum flow on a given highway segment.

The LOS for a basic freeway segment is based on the reasonable ranges for speed-flow-density on that segment. Note that density, measured in passenger cars per mile per lane, is the parameter used to define level of service for basic freeway sections. There are five levels of services, A-F, each of which is described as follows:

LOS A: Free-flow operations where the speed of an individual vehicle is controlled only by the desires of the driver and the prevailing conditions represent this level of service. There is no interference from other vehicles. The density is not greater that 10 passenger cars per mile per lane (pc/mi/ln), with an average spacing of 528 ft between consecutive vehicles. Under there conditions, an incident on the freeway may result in the lowering of the level of service at the vicinity of the incident, but quickly returns to operating at level of service A after passing the incident.

LOS B: Traffic is moving under free-flow conditions, and free-flow speeds are generally sustained. The maximum density, however, increases to 15 pc/mi/ln, with an average spacing of about 330 ft between consecutive vehicles. There are some restrictions on the ability to make lane changes or to leave or to enter the traffic stream. Drivers, however, do not find it difficult to make such maneuvers, and a high level of physical and psychological comfort is still provided to the drivers. Minor incidents can result in a more sever local deterioration than for LOS A, but the effects of minor incidents and point breakdowns are easily absorbed.

LOS C: Speeds are at or near the free-flow speed, not freedom to maneuver is noticeably restricted. Lane changes require greater vigilance by the driver, since average spacings are 220 ft (11 car lengths) at maximum density of 24 pc/mi/ln). When minor incidents increase, local deterioration in service will be substantial. Drivers experience a noticeable increase in tension because of the required added vigilance for safe operation.

LOS D: Speed begins to decline slightly with increasing flows, and density decreases somewhat more quickly. Freedom to maneuver is more noticeably limited, and drivers' experience reduced physical and psychological comfort. Vehicle spacings average 165 ft, and maximum density is 32 pc/mi/ln. Since there is little space to absorb disruptions, minor incidents can be expected to create queuing.

LOS E: Operations are volatile because there are virtually no gaps. The average spacing between consecutive vehicles decreases to 6 car lengths, with little room to maneuver at speeds still in excess of 50 mph. Maneuvers such as lane changes or merging of traffic from entrance ramps will result in a disturbance of the traffic streams. Minor incidents result in immediate and extensive queue buildup. Capacity is reached at its lower boundary, where density depends on free-flow speed.

LOS F: Operations are under breakdown conditions, and uniform moving flow cannot be maintained. These conditions prevail in queues behind the sections of freeways, with a temporary reduction in capacity. The flow conditions are such that the number of vehicles that can pass a point is less than the number of vehicles arriving at the point, or at the merging or weaving areas where the number of vehicles arriving is greater than the number discharged.[4]

A.1.2 Operational Level of Analysis

Factors of primary importance used to describe service quality for two-lane highways are average travel speed, percent time delay, as well as capacity utilization, and passing opportunities. The first two factors are of primary relevance to the current analysis.

Average travel speed is the length of the highway segment divided by the average travel time of all vehicles traveling in both directions during some designated time interval. *Percentage time delay* is the average percent of time on a given section of highway for which all vehicles are delayed while traveling in a platoon, unable to pass, typically at headways less than 5 sec. The level of service is strongly reflected in the average percent

---

[4]   Source: *Traffic and Highway Engineering*, N. J. Garber and L. A. Hoel. PWS Publishing Company, Second Edition, 1997. Pp. 336-9.

time delay. When traffic volume is low, average headways are high, demand for passing is very low, and the percent time delay tends to 0 percent. When traffic volume is very high, however, the roadway capacity is approached, and the demand for passing becomes higher than the passing capacity. This results in long platoons for traffic, and the percent time delay tends to 100 percent. The established relationships between average speed and percent time delay and volumes is often presented in a graphical manner. These relationships are presented in Figures 5 and 6.

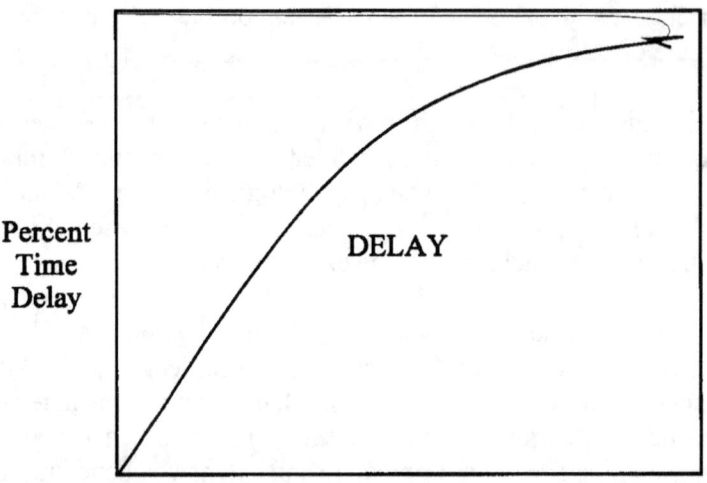

Figure 5: Relationship Between Percent Time Delay anf Flow on Two-lane Highways

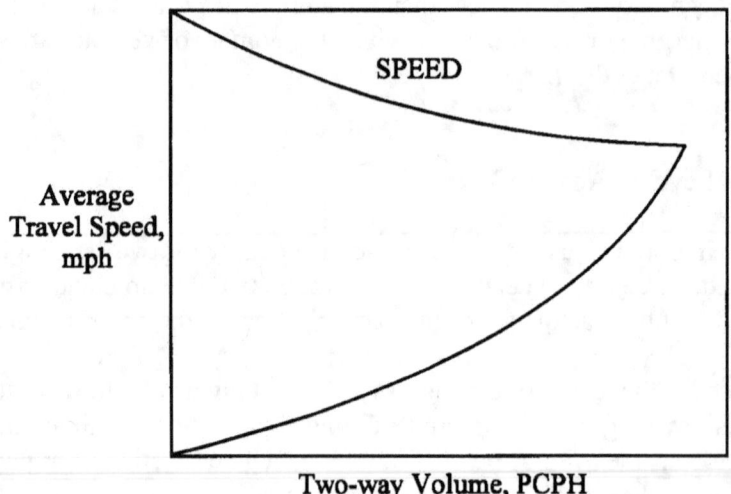

Figure 6: Relationship Between Average Speed and Flow on Two-lane Highways

These relationships are based on ideal traffic and roadway conditions. If the actual road conditions are less than ideal, the rate of traffic time delay would be higher and the travel speed would be lower than at a given traffic volume, the degree of which would depend on the conditions of the road.

A.1.3 Basic Relationship for Two-lane Highway Capacity Analysis

The service flow rate for level of service i (SF_i) is the maximum flow rate that can be maintained under prevailing conditions.

Service Flow Rate for Level of Service (LOS) i:

$$SF_i = C_j(v/c)_i(f_w)(f_{HV})(f_p)$$

Where
   Sf_i = service flow rate for level of service i under prevailing traffic and roadway
      conditions in one direction (vph)

   $(v/c)_i$ = maximum volume-to-capacity ratio for level of service i

   C_j = capacity under ideal conditions for the freeway segment having design speed
      j (2800 pc/hr/ln)

   f_w = factor to adjust for the effect of restricted lane widths and/or lateral clearance

   f_{HV} = factor to adjust for the combined effect of heavy vehicles in the traffic
      stream

where

$$f_{HV} = \frac{1}{1 + P_T(E_T - 1) + P_R(E_R - 1)}$$

   P_T, P_R = proportion of trucks/buses and RVs, respectively, in the traffic stream

   E_T, E_R = PCEs for trucks/buses and RVs, respectively (PCE: passenger car
      equivalent)

   f_p = factor to adjust for the effect of recreational or unfamiliar driver populations

This measurement is used determine the current road traffic conditions and the prediction for the next 10 years given the potential traffic growth rate in the area (Port Fourchon) for 27 highway segments (based on DOTD highway control number). These 27 segments accounted for the total of 78.5 miles.[5] Also, the changes of LOS for these segments are estimated based on low and high traffic growth rates in the future.[6]

---

[5]   One section of road, extending from Golden Meadow to Cutoff, was excluded from analysis. This
      section was excluded because it is presently scheduled to be widened.

[6]   These estimates are presented in a later section.

A.1.4 Ranking of Pavement Condition

The Rational Factorial Ranking Method (FRM) uses a priority index that combines climatic conditions, traffic, roughness, and distress to rank the current conditions of a highway, and, therefore, can be used to determine the needs for improvement. The priority index is expressed as:

$$Y = 5.4\,(0.0263X_1) - (0.0132X_2) - [0.4\log(X_3)] + (0.749X_4) + (1.66X_5)$$

where

> Y = The priority index ranges from 1 to 10, with 1 representing very poor, and 10 representing excellent. Thus a low value indicates a pavement which should receive a high priority for treatment.
>
> X_1 = average rainfall (in./yr)
>
> X_2 = freeze and thaw (cycle/yr)
>
> X_3 = Traffic (AADT)
>
> X_4 = present serviceability index
>
> X_5 = distress (a subjective number between -1 and $+1$)

A.2 Experimental Findings

This section includes the sources of data used in this study and empirical results based on the traffic and other relevant information.

A.2.1 Data sources

The data used in this analysis include:

a. Traffic and road condition data from Louisiana Department of Transportation and Development (DOTD): *Highway Needs Study Inventory Form* for total of 27 segments, 78.5 miles of highway data;

b. Historic average daily traffic (ADT) data from 1973 to 1997, for 6 sections (DOTD data);

c. Two months daily hour traffic counting data, with detailed information pertaining to the different vehicle types from the Port Fourchon Commission;

d. Truck flow data in and out of Port Fourchon for the 1994-97 calendar years from several of the major for- hire and independent trucking companies servicing the Port Fourchon area[7].

A.2.2 Results

The empirical results are presented in four sections. In the first section, the current traffic and road conditions for the two-lane rural highways which lead to Port Fourchon are examined. Then, the average daily traffic change patterns over the last 25 years (1973 – 1997) are presented. In the third section, predicted traffic flows and their possible influence on future traffic conditions is presented. Finally, the current pavement conditions of the two-lane highways are analyzed.

A.2.2.1 The current traffic flow and road conditions

The data provided by DOTD in Table 3 (on the following page following page) documents the current traffic and road conditions. The sections associated with each of the four digit numbers are listed below[8] In addition, each of the sections is further divided into several subsections of road. For purposes of this report, however, discussion is generally limited to just the aggregate sections which are:

    6401: Grand Isle area
    6402: Leeville – La3090 (Port Fourchon)
    6490: Golden Meadow – Leeville
    6405: Lockport – Cut-Off
    6406: Raceland - Lockport
    6407 and 6408: North of Raceland

A.2.2.2 The weighted ADT for consideration

The weighted ADT for the 78.5 miles of Highway 1 considered in the analysis equaled almost 7,400 when combining all sections but varied considerably depending on the section of road being evaluated. In general, the ADT declined when moving in a southernly direction along the highway.

---

[7] To determine the average annual growth in truck traffic in and out of Port Fourchon, the major for-hire trucking firms that serviced the Port Fourchon area, as well as other independent truck firms out of the Houston area, were surveyed. These trucking firms were asked to provide information pertaining to annual change in Port Fourchon operations during the 1994-97 period. In some instances, firms released to the researchers actual records for all or part of the 1994-97 period. If a firm was unable (or unwilling) to provide actual records, it was asked to estimate growth. Results associated with this survey are discussed in the Deterioration section of this report.

[8] Section 6404, i.e., that section of Highway 1 extending from Golden Meadow to Cutoff was, as previously noted, not included in the analysis because it is scheduled to be four laned.

Table 3: Current Traffic and Road Conditions

Place	Section Code	Length (miles)	ADT	PSR	LOS	Avg. travel speed (m/h)	Avg. HWY speed (m/h)	Recomm. type of improvement
Grand Isle area	640101	1.42	452	2.7	a	45	60	c
	640102	5.12	3900	2.8	b	45	70	d
	640103	0.7	3483	2.8	b	55	70	a
	640104	2.47	3483	3.0	b	57	70	d
	6401	*9.71*	*3260*	*2.8*		*49*	*69*	
Leesville - LA3090	640201	6.3	2085	2.9	a	58	70	d
	640202	6.99	4245	4.0	b	56	70	j
	6402	*13.29*	*3221*	*3.5*		*57*	*70*	
Golden Meadow - Leesville	649001	0.5	7576	2.9	d	41	35	a
	649002	4.5	7576	2.7	c	52	70	i
	649003	4.33	7576	2.9	d	45	70	i
	649004	1.6	7576	3.6	d	30	50	i
	6490	*10.93*	*7576*	*2.9*		*46*	*65*	
Lockport - Cut-Off	640501	3.28	5703	2.8	a	42	45	i
	640502	0.39	5703	2.3	a	41	45	a
	640503	1.02	5703	2.3	c	25	35	i
	640504	9.64	6332	2.1	c	54	70	i
	6405	*14.33*	*6126*	*2.3*		*49*	*61*	
Raceland - Lockport	640601	1.4	2512	2.6	c	35	60	i
	640602	0.08	5812	2.4	c	35	60	a
	640603	4.99	9476	2.4	e	45	60	e
	640604	0.32	10801	3.7	b	45	70	i
	640605	2.14	10801	4.0	f	14	45	e
	6406	*8.93*	*8716*	*2.9*		*36*	*57*	
North of Raceland	640701	0.2	8447	3.5	a	26	30	i
	640702	7.22	13125	4.0	d	50	70	e
	640703	5.8	13125	3.8	d	50	70	e
	640704	1.01	7519	4.0	c	22	35	e
	640705	0.48	8419	3.6	e	10	25	e
	6407	*14.71*	*12523*	*3.9*		*46*	*66*	
	640801	0.29	14308	2.8	f	2	25	e
	640802	0.68	14102	3.7	f	1	35	e
	640803	5.63	9604	3.8	d	51	70	e
	6408	*6.6*	*10274*	*3.7*		*44*	*64*	
	Total	*78.5*	*7387*	*3.1*		*40*	*57*	

The sections of road above Raceland (i.e., sections 6407 and 6408), for example, indicated ADT's in excess of 10 thousand. The sections of road from Leeville to Grand Isle, by comparison, indicated ADT's of only slightly more than three thousand, or less than a third of the observed ADT's along the northern stretch of the

16

road. A particularly pronounced decline in ADT was evident South of Leeville.

In general, the current traffic performance level, measured as LOS, is in fair condition when evaluated on the basis of DODT data. As described earlier, a higher level of service translates into better traffic conditions (as LOS approaches A), while the lower level of service translates into worse traffic conditions (as LOS approaches F). The weighted average LOS based on the length of each of the segments (total weight is 78.5) is presented in Figure 7. As indicated, 57% of the road has a level of service of at least C, i.e., of average condition or better, while 43% of the 78.5 mile stretch of road is in a condition below average (LOS D, E, F). In general, the level of service is highest in the Grand Isle area (i.e., section 6401) but deteriorates as one moves north on the highway (see Table 3). The 10.9-mile section of road between Golden Meadow and Leeville, however, offers a very low level of service (i.e., the LOS along all subsections of section 6490 are below the level of C).

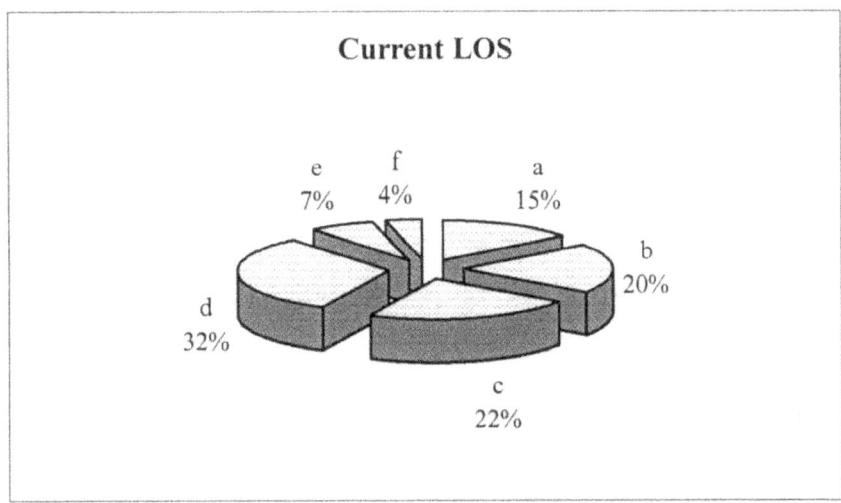

Figure 7: Proportion of Current LOS

PSR, *present serviceability rating*, a measurement of pavement condition, is a number given to a pavement section based on the ability of that pavement to serve its intended traffic. DOTD uses a rating system as depicted in Table 4 to evaluate pavement conditions.

Table 4: DOTD Rating System	
PSR	**RATING**
0 - 2.0	Very Poor
2.1 - 2.5	Poor
2.6 - 3.4	Fair
3.5 - 3.9	Good
4.0 - 5.0	Very Good

The current PSR for the 27 subsections of pavement used in the current analysis ranges from a low of 2.1 to a high of 4. Currently, almost 60% of the 78.5 miles highway has a poor or fair pavement condition, while 22% (24 miles) and 19% (i.e., 14 miles) of the 78.5 miles of pavement is in very good or good condition, respectively (see Figure 8 below).

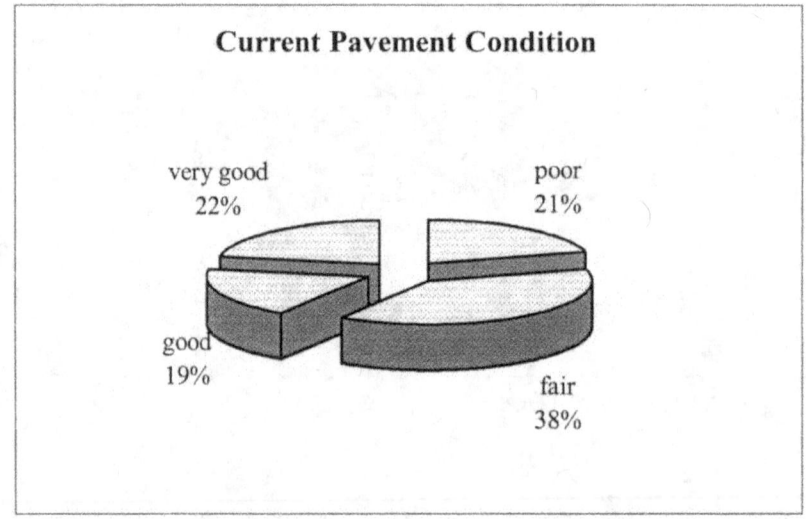

Current Pavement Condition

very good 22%
poor 21%
good 19%
fair 38%

Figure 8: Current Pavement Condition

Overall, the average travel speed along the 78.5-mile stretch of Highway 1 used in the current analysis was estimated to equal 40 mph, which is approximately 30% below the intended average highway speed of 57 mph. For the two road sections of closest proximity to Port Fourchon (i.e., section 6402 extending from Leeville to LA 3090 and section 6490 which extends from Golden Meadow to Leeville), the average travel speeds are 19% and 12% below the intended highway average speeds. From Raceland to Lockport, the actual average driving speed is close to 40% below the intended speed. These figures suggest that, on average, driving conditions are well below "optimal". With low travel speed, furthermore, it is expected that a higher than normal percent time delay would be encountered (again, refer to Figures 5 and 6).

The "recommended" types of improvement are part of a DOTD highway improvement plan based on the over-all road conditions. The different types of improvement are presented in Table 5, below.

Table 5: Improvement Types and Recommendations	
Improvement Type	Description
a	No Improvement
b	New Location
c	Reconstruction
d	Isolated Reconstruction
e	Major Widening
f	Minor Widening
g	Minor Widening and Isolated Reconstruction
h	Resurfacing and Isolated Reconstruction
i	Resurfacing
l	Resealing

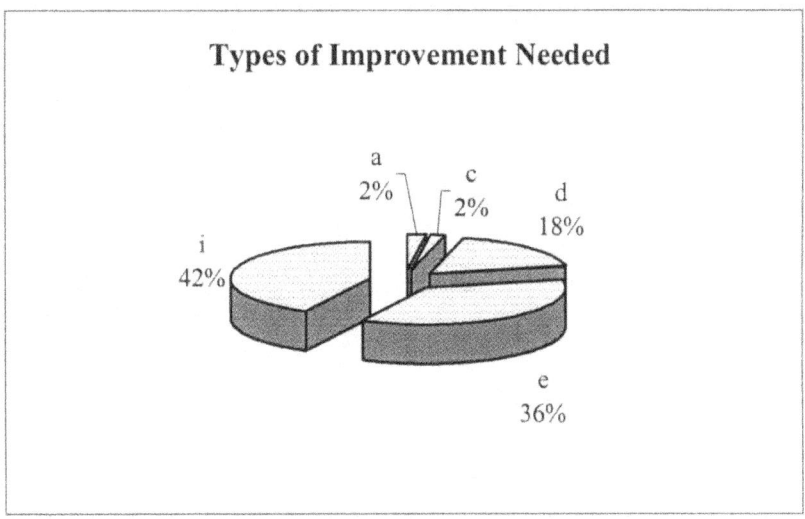

Figure 9: Types of Improvement Needed

The information contained in Figure 9 (preceeding page) suggests that, at present,

19

most of the 78.5-mile section of Highway 1 used in the analysis requires some kind of improvement (only 2% of the road is not recommended for improvement). Overall, 36% of the 78.5-mile stretch of road needs major widening (e), and another 42% needs resurfacing (i).

A.2.2.3 The Average Daily Traffic Growth Pattern For 1973-97 And Anticipated Change

The traffic growth trend along the 78.5-mile stretch of Highway 1 fluctuated widely during the 25- year period ending in 1997. The growth rates in ADT for selected periods during the 1973-97 period are illustrated in Figure 10.

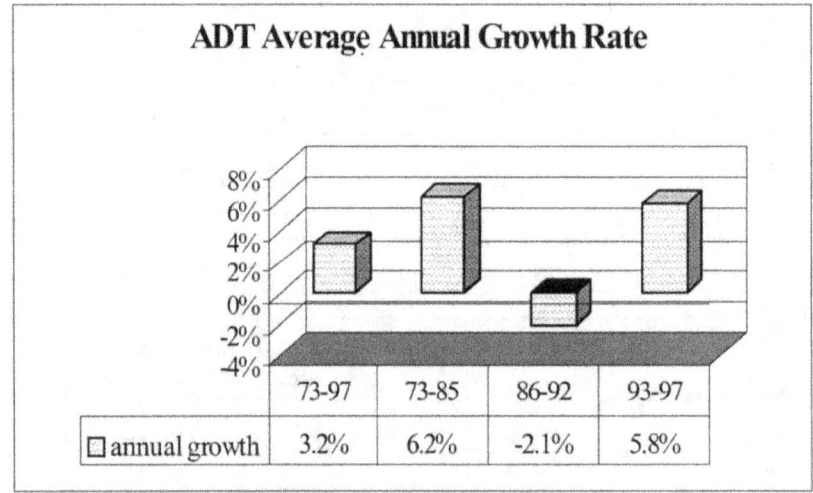

Figure 10: ADT Average Annual Growth Rate

As indicated, the growth rate in ADT along the 78.5-mile stretch of Highway 1 equaled 3.2% per year when evaluated over the 25-year period of analysis ending in 1997. This growth rate, as mentioned, fluctuated widely depending upon the time period considered. During the 1973-85 period, for example, the annual growth rate exceeded the six percent rate. During the 1986-92 period, by comparison, the growth rate was actually negative (i.e., -2.1% per year). Finally, the annual growth rate approached the six percent mark again during the 1973-97 period; a growth rate comparable to that recorded by DODT during 1973-85.

ADT on a given section(s) of road, as one might expect, tends to be related to economic activities in the region. Simply stated, as economic activities expand in a given region, increased transportation along the road system in that region will be forthcoming. Hence, the demand for road services will expand in direct relation to the level of economic activities.

While somewhat speculative in the absence of a more in depth analysis, ADT changes along Highway 1 appear to be significantly influenced by the overall level of economic activities. Furthermore, much of these economic activities appear to be oil-

and-gas based. The 1973-85 period, for example, can be characterized as expanding (or at least a relatively high level) oil-and-gas activities. Specifically, oil prices, following the OPEC embargo in 1973, began a long upward trend which stimulated domestic oil-and-gas activities in the region. In 1970, for instance, the wellhead price for a barrel of oil equaled $3.18 (McKenzie et al., 1993). By 1980, the price had risen to in excess of $21 per barrel and approached $32 per barrel in 1981. Though declining somewhat after 1981, prices remained at about the $24 mark or above until 1986. In 1986, however, the price fell to $12.45 per barrel. This represented about a 50% decline when compared to the 1985 price of $24.08. The impact of this price decline was immediate. As one indication of the impact, the number of exploratory wells drilled in the Central and Western Gulf of Mexico OCS fell from 483 in 1985 to 260 in 1986, a decline of almost 50% (McKenzie et al., 1993).

Overall, the 6.2% annual growth rate along Highway 1 during the 1973-85 period appears to closely mirror the expanding or relatively strong oil-and-gas activities during the period. Similarly, the sharp decline in ADT after 1985 and through 1992 appears to mirror the sharp decline in oil-and-gas and overall economic activities in the region during that time period. While there is less evidence to directly link the growth in ADT during the 1993-97 to expanding oil-and-gas activities, such a relationship, at least in part, appears plausible. This later relationship is, however, somewhat tentative.

Overall, the above discussion highlights the fact that ADT along Highway 1 appears to be heavily influenced by the level of oil-and-gas activities. Furthermore, if expansion in oil-and-gas activities generate economic activities comparable to those observed during the 1973-85 period, annual growth rate in ADT could well approach the six percent mark. For forecasting purposes, therefore, a six percent growth rate in ADT during the next ten years is given as an upper bound estimate. As a lower-bound estimate a three percent ADT growth rate during the next ten years is assumed. These two bounds appear appropriate in light of historical and current data revealing trends in ADT along Highway 1.[9]

The ten-year projections of ADT growth based on the lower and upper bound estimates provide above are presented in Figure 11.[10] With a six percent ADT growth rate during the next decade, average daily traffic will exceed 13 thousand along the 78.5-mile stretch

---

[9] The high-end forecast (i.e., six percent growth rate in ADT) is, of course, based on the premises that: (1) OCS and, particularly, the deepwater activities in the Central Gulf of Mexico continue at a strong pace during the next decade and (2) that Port Fourchon remains a central hub of support services to these expanding activities. At present, no information exists to suggest that these premises are not realistic. If realistic, the three percent lower-bound estimate of ADT growth over the next decade, based on historical information, may well be overly conservative.

[10] In terms of traffic flow, one truck is equivalent to approximately 2.2 passenger cars. From the counter data located at Port Fourchon, the proportion of trucks was found to equal 13%. This figure was used in the calculation of ADT. While the percentage of trucks is expected to increase in relation to expanding offshore oil-and-gas activities in the Central Gulf of Mexico, no attempt was made to include this expected increase in truck traffic in the estimation of future growth in ADT.

of Highway 1 used in the analysis, an increase of approximately 80% when compared to 7.4 thousand ADT recorded in 1997.

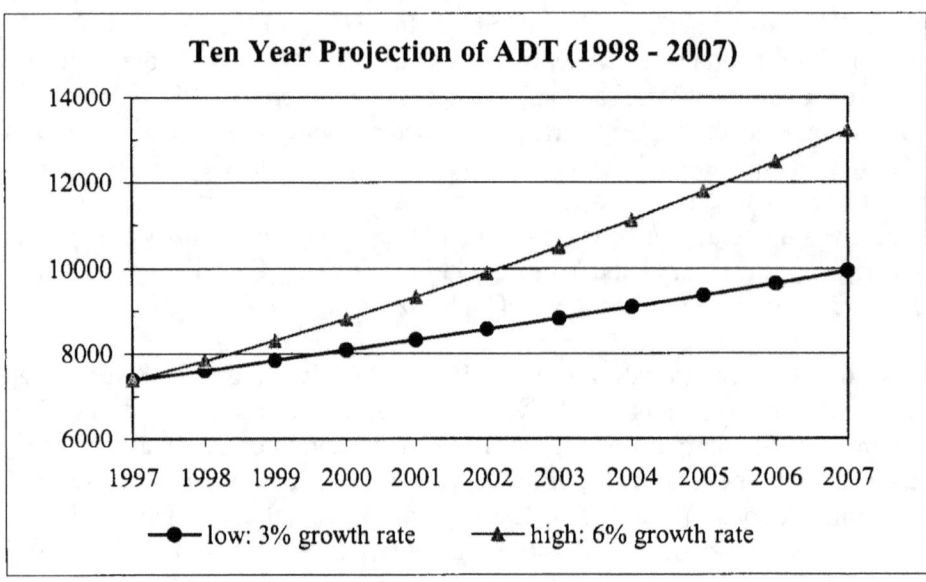

Figure 11: Ten Year Projection of ADT (1998-2007)

Under the scenerio of a three percent average annual growth rate during the next decade (i.e., the lower-bound estimate), daily traffic along the 78.5-mile stretch of Highway 1 will approach 10 thousand by the year 2007, an increase of almost 35%. While sufficient information does not exist to predict the actual future change with a greater level of precision, it will likely fall somewhere in between the lower and upper bound estimates. Furthermore, regardless of the exact figure, it is evident that expansion in OCS activities in the Central Gulf of Mexico will increasingly strain the ability of Highway 1 to provide an "adequate" level of services needed in support of these expanding offshore oil-and-gas activities.[11]

A.2.2.3.1 The predicted traffic flows and it's affects on future traffic conditions:

The increasing traffic flow associated with expanding offshore oil-and-gas activities can be used to ascertain anticipated changes in LOS by the year 2007. These changes, based on the two growth rate scenerios are presented in Figures 12 (i.e., three percent growth rate) and 13 (i.e., six percent growth rate).

---

[11]   While outside of the scope of the present study, it is worth mentioning that the increased traffic volume along LA 1 will, most likely, result in an increasing number of accidents, injuries, and fatalities.

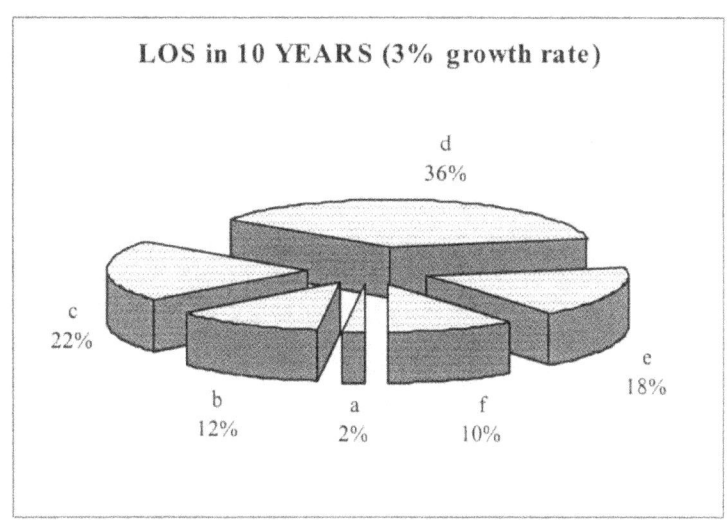

Figure 12: Predicted Traffic Flow in Year 2007 Based on a Three-
Percent Growth Rate

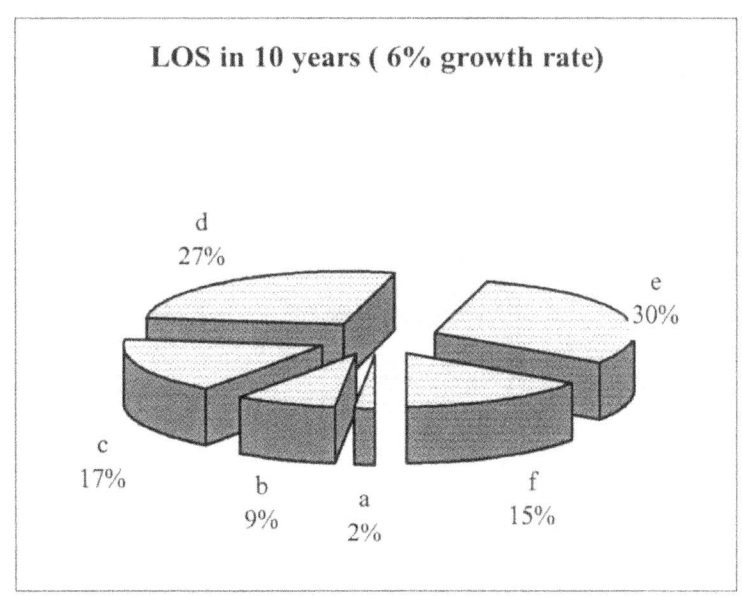

Figure 13: Predicted Traffic Flow in Year 2007 Based on a Six-
Percent Growth Rate

With an assumed three percent growth rate in ADT during the next decade, the proportion
of the highway providing a level of service A (very good traffic conditions) will equal
only two percent in the year 2007 (Figure 12). This is significantly below the current
proportion of 15% (see Figure 7). Similarly, the proportion of the 78.5-mile stretch of
Highway 1 receiving a LOS equal to B will fall from 20% to only 12%. At the other
extreme, the LOS equal to D will increase from 32% to 36%, the LOS equal to E will
advance from only seven percent to almost 20%, and the LOS equal to F will more than
double from four percent to 10%. As suggested by the definitions associated with these

different levels of service (LOS), any LOS equal to a D or below tends to suggest relatively "significant" traffic flow patterns. Overall, the proportion of highway with a level of service equal to D or less, under the context of a three percent growth rate in ADT, advances from 43% in 1997 to 64% by 2007.

Given the upper-bound estimate of six percent annual growth in ADT during the next decade, the proportion of highway exhibiting a level of service equal to D or below will advance to more than 70% (see Figure 13), an increase of approximately 60% from the observed 1997 levels. Conversely, the proportion of the highway which would be characterized as either A or B would fall from the current figure of 35% to only 11%. These estimates, in general, suggest some rather serious capacity problems along Highway 1 if the upper-bound estimates of ADT are realized over the next decade.

Summarization of predicted changes in LOS by the year 2007 under the lower bound and higher bound ADT growth estimates is presented in Figure 14. Overall deterioration in the level of service offered is, as indicated, significant within the context of both the three percent and six percent growth scenerios.

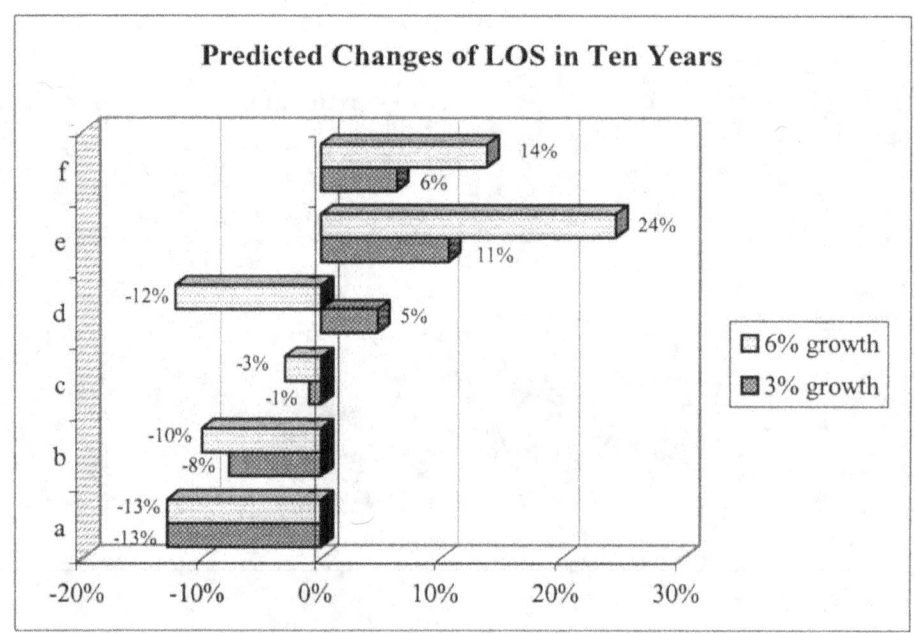

Figure 14: Predicted Changes is LOS in Ten Years Based on Projected Growth Rates of Three- and Six-Percent

In general, the change in LOS under the two different growth rate scenerios depends heavily on the segment of highway being considered. In the Grand Isle area (i.e., section 6401), for example, the estimated LOS declines only marginally by 2007 even with the assumed six percent growth rate during the next decade. Specifically, all four subsections along this stretch of road will maintain a level of service equal to fair or better (i.e., LOS equal to C or above). By contrast, all subsections of road along the Lockport to Cut Off (i.e., section 6405) stretch currently exhibit a LOS of A through C indicating fair to very

24

good road services. With a three percent growth rate over the next decade, all subsections along this stretch will exhibit a LOS of D and at a six percent growth rate, all subsections of the stretch of road would exhibit a LOS equal to E.

A.2.2.3.2 Analysis of current pavement conditions

The approach of Rational Factorial Ranking Method (FRM) is used to evaluate the current pavement condition. As noted, the FRM can be expressed as:

$$Y = 5.4 \, (0.0263X_1) - (0.0132X_2) - [0.4\log(X_3)] + (0.749X_4) + (1.66X_5)$$

For purposes of analysis, the variable X1 (i.e., annual average rainfall in Lafourche Parish) was set at 80.9. Since no freeze/cycles are generally observed in Lafourche Parish, the value of X2 was set equal to zero. The actual 1997 ADT values associated with the 27 subsections of pavement (i.e., 78.5 miles) were used to estimate a value for X3. Similarly, the DODT data on the 27 subsections of pavement were utilized to develop an estimate of the present serviceability index (X4). Finally, the distress index (X5), as noted, can range from +1 to -1. Choice of the value to employ for estimation purposes is subjective. Because of the subjective nature of this variable, values of both 0 and -1 were utilized in the estimation of the FRM equation.[12]

Results associated with the FRM estimation procedure are presented in Figure 15 on the following page. The shorter bars represent low possible rankings for the current pavement condition (i.e., the distress value was set to –1) The longer bars represent rankings associated with the more liberal distress value (i.e., the distress value was set to 0). The highest possible rank which can be attained based on the FRM expression is a 10 suggesting that the pavement is in excellent condition. None of the 27 subsections of pavement, as indicated by the information contained in Figure 15, approach the index of five (based on a value of either 0 or -1 associated with the distress index). For example, if considering the distress value –1, eleven sections have an index value below 2.5 (sections in 6405, 6406, 6408 and 6490, between Leeville and Raceland), implying that improvements should receive high priority. All other sections received an index value of less than 3 (under distress value –1).

With a three percent ADT growth rate, the average road quality will deteriorate by approximately 16% (based on the distress factor being set to zero) during the next decade as measured by the FRM.[13] When the distress factor is set to -1, the road quality deteriorates, on average, by more than 25%. In general, only minor differences in road quality , as measured by the FRM expression, were apparent when comparing the three percent and six percent ADT growth rates.

---

[12]   Given the relatively high truck volume along LA 1, a value of +1 was not considered in the estimation of the FRM expression.

[13]   This estimate should be considered a minimum because the value of x4 has been held constant. As ADT increases over time, one would expect to see a decline in present serviceability index.

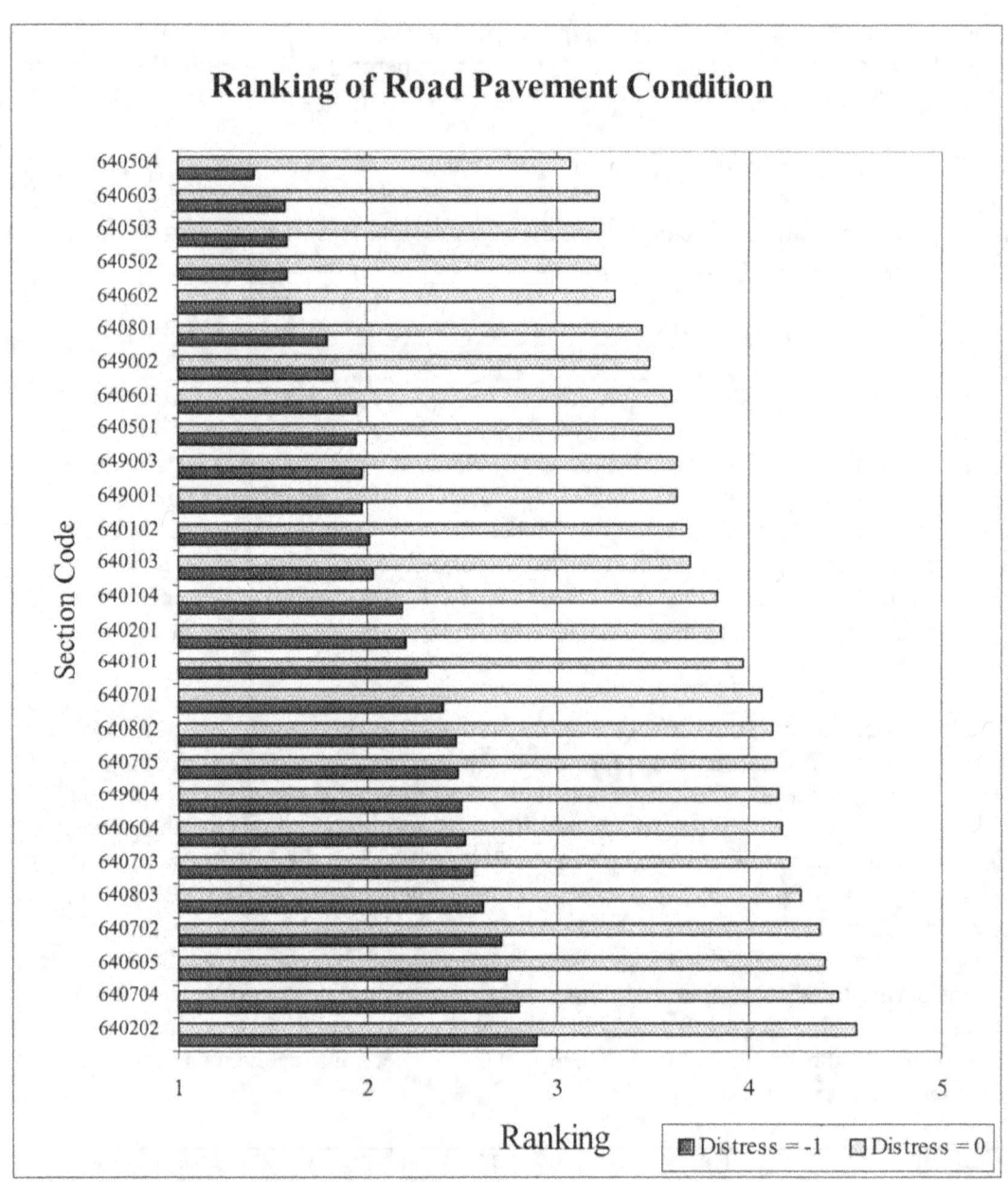

Figure 15: Ranking of Road Pavement Condition

B. Highway Deterioration Analysis for Port Fourchon

Highway pavement consists of either rigid pavement or flexible pavement. Flexible pavement, as is the pavement of Highway 1, is usually a bituminous surface underlaid by a layer of granular material that is in turn underlaid by a layer consisting of a mixture of coarse and fine materials (Garber and Hoel 1997). Weather and vehicle level stress are the major factors in determining road wear. Because the effects of weather do not differ within a given region, road vehicle level can be especially important in determining highway design and life. For such a vehicle level, vertical (compressive) stress from a wheel load is distributed throughout the pavement as horizontal (tensile) stress. Vertical compressive stress at the surface of the subgrade layer and horizontal tensile strain at the bottom of the asphalt layer are the critical criteria (Garber and Hoel 1997).

Thickness and stiffness of the pavement levels are the critical factors in the ability to withstand stress due to wheel load. Hence, the major principle of design procedure is determining the minimum thickness of the asphalt layer that can adequately withstand vertical and horizontal stresses over the life of the road (before replacement). Stresses are, of course, a function of wheel load and wheel load is in turn determined by the distributed weight of the vehicle traveling on the road (Garber and Hoel 1997).

The stress placed by vehicles on pavement is reported in terms of the number of repetitions of an 18,000 lb single-axle load applied to the pavement by two sets of dual tires, or the equivalent single axle load (ESAL). Repeated experiments have demonstrated that the effect of any load on pavement performance can be translated into the number of ESALs. The dual tires are depicted by two circular plates, both 4.51 inches in diameter and 13.57 inches apart, which results in a contact pressure of 70 pound per inch (Garber and Hoel 1997).

Several different estimates of ESAL by vehicle type are available. Load equivalency factors by weight and by type of axle (single, tandem, and tridem) are reported in Table 6 on the following page (The Asphalt Institute, 1991). While such information is useful, it is not directly applicable because not all vehicles are fully loaded in weight terms. In other words, vehicles are often at full capacity in terms of volume, but are not at full capacity in terms of weight. Further, although back hauling is the norm, many trucks are empty in return trips. Nationally derived estimates of ESAL generated by trucks that account for weight load levels typically found on various types of roads are provided in Table 7 (second page following). These national values were not used in this study, however. Rather, data generated by the Louisiana Department of Transportation and Economic Development (DOTD) based on Louisiana conditions were used in this study. These estimates of ESAL generated over vehicles, which account for the average weight per vehicle, are provided in Table 8 (third page following). It is important to point out that relatively light weight vehicles, such as passenger cars, generate negligible ESALs as compared to heavier vehicles. It is also important to note that for heavier vehicles, such as trucks with five or more axles, the estimates of ESAL generated that are used in this study

Table 6: Load Equivalency Factors

Gross Axle Load		Load Equivalency Factors			Gross Axle Load		Load Equivalency Factors		
kN	lb	Single Axles	Tandem Axles	Tridem Axles	kN	lb	Single Axles	Tandem Axles	Tridem Axles
4.45	1 k	0.00002			204.5	46 k	37.24	3.55	0.868
8.9	2 k	0.00018			213.5	48 k	44.50	4.17	1.033
17.8	4 k	0.00209	0.0003		222.4	50 k	52.88	4.86	1.22
26.7	6 k	0.01043	0.001	0.0003	231.3	52 k		5.63	1.43
35.6	8 k	0.0343	0.003	0.001	240.2	54 k		6.47	1.66
44.5	10 k	0.0877	0.007	0.002	249.0	56 k		7.41	1.91
53.4	12 k	0.189	0.014	0.003	258.0	58 k		8.45	2.20
62.3	14 k	0.360	0.027	0.006	267.0	60 k		9.59	2.51
71.2	16 k	0.623	0.047	0.011	275.8	62 k		10.84	2.85
80.0	18 k	1.000	0.077	0.017	284.5	64 k		12.22	3.22
89.0	20 k	1.51	0.121	0.027	293.5	66 k		13.73	3.62
97.9	22 k	2.18	0.180	0.040	302.5	68 k		15.38	4.05
106.8	24 k	3.03	0.260	0.057	311.5	70 k		17.19	4.52
115.6	26 k	4.09	0.364	0.080	320.0	72 k		19.16	5.03
124.5	28 k	5.39	0.495	0.109	329.0	74 k		21.32	5.57
133.4	30 k	6.97	0.658	0.145	338.0	76 k		23.66	6.15
142.3	32 k	8.88	0.857	0.191	347.0	78 k		26.22	6.78
151.2	34 k	11.18	1.095	0.246	356.0	80 k		29.0	7.45
160.1	36 k	13.93	1.39	0.313	364.7	82 k		32.0	8.2
169.0	38 k	17.20	1.70	0.393	373.6	84 k		35.3	8.9
178.0	40 k	21.08	2.08	0.487	382.5	86 k		38.8	9.8
187.0	42 k	25.64	2.51	0.597	391.4	88 k		42.6	10.6
195.7	44 k	31.00	3.00	0.723	400.3	90 k		46.8	11.6

Note: kN converted to lb are within 0.1 percent of lb shown.
Source: *Thickens Design - Asphalt Pavements for Highways and Streets*, Manual Series No. 1, The Asphalt Institute, Lexington, Ky., February 1991.

Table 7: Distribution of Truck Factors for Different Classes of Highways and Vehicles

Vehicle Type:	Rural Systems						Urban Systems		All Systems	
	Interstate Rural		Other Rural		All Rural		All Urban			
	Average	Range	Average	Range	Average	Range	Average	Range	Average	Range
Single-unit Trucks										
2-axle, 4-tire	0.02	0.01 - 0.06	0.02	0.01 - 0.09	0.03	0.02 - 0.08	0.03	0.01 - 0.05	0.02	0.01 - 0.07
2-axle, 6-tire	0.19	0.13 - 0.30	0.21	0.14 - 0.34	0.20	0.14 - 0.31	0.26	0.18 - 0.42	0.21	0.15 - 0.32
3-axle or more	0.56	0.09 - 1.55	0.73	0.31 - 1.57	0.67	0.23 - 1.53	0.13	0.52 - 1.99	0.73	0.29 - 1.59
All single-units	0.07	0.02 - 0.16	0.07	0.02 - 0.17	0.07	0.03 - 0.16	0.09	0.04 - 0.21	0.07	0.02 - 0.17
Tractor Semi-trailers										
3-axle	0.51	0.30 - 0.86	0.47	0.29 - 0.82	0.48	0.31 - 0.80	0.47	0.24 - 1.02	0.48	0.33 - 0.78
4-axle	0.62	0.40 - 1.07	0.83	0.44 - 1.55	0.70	0.37 - 1.34	0.89	0.60 - 1.64	0.73	0.43 - 1.32
5-axle or more[1]	0.94	0.67 - 1.15	0.98	0.58 - 1.70	0.95	0.58 - 1.64	1.02	0.69 - 1.69	0.95	0.63 - 1.53
All multiple units	0.93	0.67 - 1.38	0.97	0.67 - 1.50	0.94	0.66 - 1.43	1.00	0.72 - 1.58	0.95	0.71 - 1.39
All trucks	0.49	0.34 - 0.77	0.31	0.20 - 0.52	0.42	0.29 - 0.67	0.30	0.15 - 0.59	0.40	0.27 - 0.63

Note: [1] Including full-trailer combinations in some states.
Source: Compiled from data supplied by the Highway Statistics Division, U.S. Federal Highway Administration

Table 8: Vehicle Factors Used in Estimating ESALs in Study of Impact of Vehicle Use on Highway 1 in Lafouche Parish		
Vehicle Classification	Description	Equivalency Factors
1	Motorcycles	0.0005
2	Passenger Cars	0.0005
3	Other Two-Axle, Four-Tire, Single-Unit Vehicles	0.0188
4	Buses	0.1932
5	Two-Axle, Six-Tire, Single-Unit Trucks	0.1932
6	Three-Axle, Single-Unit Trucks	0.4095
7	Four-or-More-Axle, Single-Unit Trucks	0.4095
8	Four-or-Less-Axle, Single-Trailer Trucks	0.8814
9	Five-Axle, Single-Trailer Trucks	1.1000
10	Six-or-More-Axle, Single-Trailer Trucks	1.4500
11	Five-or-Less Axle, Multi-Trailer Truck	1.8400
12	Six-Axle, Multi-Trailer Trucks	1.8400
13	Seven-or-More-Axle, Multi-Trailer Truck	1.8400
Source: Louisiana Department of Transportation and Development, *Design Manual*. Unpublished, Baton Rouge, 1993.		

(Table 8) are markedly lower than the estimates of ESAL generated from national data (as shown in Table 7). This difference occurs because the national data is based on number of axle, while the data used in this study are based on type of truck. Hence, the values presented in this study can be considered to be conservative in this respect.

The highway design period is the number of years that pavement can continue to carry the traffic load without needing a new overlay (repavement). For flexible highway pavement, the design period is usually 20 years. However, heavy use can cause adjustments in the design period. Because traffic volume usually increases over time, it is important to determine the traffic growth rates, especially for trucks, over the design period. Once the growth rate has been determined, the design lane must be established that is used in either determining pavement thickness need or in projecting when a new overlay would be needed. For a two-lane highway, either lane can be the design lane. Its identification is important, because in some cases truck traffic will be greater in one direction or because trucks may tend to carry loads in one direction and be empty in the other direction. Given these factors, a general equation has been constructed for

30

accumulated ESAL, by the ith axle load category or:

$$ESAL_i = f_d \ X \ G_{jt} \ \ X \ ADDT_i \ X \ 365 \ X \ N_i \ X \ F_{ei} \qquad (4)$$

where:

ESAL$_i$ = the equivalent accumulated 18,000 lb single-axle load for the ith axle category

f_d = the design lane factor (percent of total category traffic in the design lane)

G_{jt} = the traffic growth factor for a given growth rate j and design period t

ADDT$_i$ = the first year, annual average daily traffic for the ith axle category

N_i = the number of axles in each vehicle in the ith category

F_{ei} = the load equivalency factor for the ith axle category

Over all axle categories (I=1.....n) the total accumulated ESAL is given by:

$$ESAL = \sum_{I=1}^{n} ESAL_i \qquad (5)$$

The subgrade is also important in determining the ability of a road to bear traffic. The subgrade is made up of either natural soil or soil imported to form an embankment. The most important soil property relating to bearing capacity is the resilient modulus, "which gives the resilient characteristic of the soil when it is repeatedly loaded with ESAL equivalent axial load" (p.936, Garber and Hoel 1997).

If the subgrade resilient modulus and the ESAL are known, then the thickness of the asphalt layer can be calculated assuming a 20 year service period. Determining the effect of current and future road use on a current highway may be more problematic.

As previously stated, the ability of a road to withstand any particular level of use can be measured by thicknesses and stiffness of the pavement layers and the quality of the subsurface. This reduces to estimating the current thickness of the asphalt layers and the resiliency of the support base to accommodate a given amount of cumulative road stress over a period of time (the number of design years), as measured by cumulative number of ESAL. The roadbed soil resilient modulus (M factor) is measured in pounds per square inch. The M factor for soils in Lafourche parish is 9,000 psi as estimated by the Louisiana DOTD.[14]

As based on data provided by the Louisiana DOTD, thickness of the asphalt layer was estimated for four stretches of Highway 1, all in Lafouche Parish south of Golden

---

[14]A reviewer of this report suggested that the M factor used in this study (i.e., 9,000 psi) may be somewhat inflated. If this is the case, the estimates concerning when overlays will be needed will be unduly conservative suggesting that overlays will be required at a date closer to the present.

Meadow in one-tenth of a mile increments. Thickness of the asphalt layer was estimated at a average of 8.1 for a 5.9 mile long section (064021a) of Highway 1, at nine inches for a 7.4 mile section (064021b), at six inches for a 9.2 mile section (064901a), and at 6.0 inches for 1.7 mile section (064901b) as depicted in Table 9 below. Standard deviations, and minimum and maximum thickness estimates for each of the four sections are provided in Table 9.

Table 9: Statistics for Asphalt Layer Thickness, for Four Sections of Road Used in Estimating the Need to Repave Highway 1.						
Road Section	Last Repavement (Year)	Length (Miles)	Mean Thickness (Inches)	Standard Deviation (Inches)	Maximum Thickness (Inches)	Minimum Thickness (Inches)
064021a	1981	5.9	8.13	1.14	10.60	6.20
064021b	1993	7.4	9.08	1.17	11.40	5.50
064901a	1979	9.2	6.21	0.33	7.10	5.70
064901b	1994	1.7	6.02	0.61	5.30	7.20
Source: Louisiana Department of Transportation and Development (DOTD), Baton Rouge, 1997. All road thickness values estimated by DOTD in 1995.						

Design charts for pavement with an asphalt concrete surface (Garber and Hoel) were then used to estimate the number of cumulative ESAL (design number if ESAL) for the four sections of road. The design number of ESAL is the maximum number of ESAL that a section of road can be expected to sustain without major rework. For the section (064021a) with an average asphalt layer thickness of 8.1 inches, the design number of ESAL was estimated at 2.3 million. For the section (064021b) with an average asphalt layer thickness of 9.1 inches, the design number of ESAL was estimated at 3.0 million. For the sections with an average asphalt layer thickness of 6.2 inches (064901a) and 6.0 inches (064901b), the design number of ESAL was estimated to be 1.2 million and 1.1 million. All four figures provided an estimate of the traffic bearing capacity of the two sections of Highway 1, given that current and future traffic--in terms of ESAL--can be estimated.

ESAL estimates were obtained based on traffic counter data. Daily (24 hour) traffic data was collected starting on July 31 through September 28 for 40 days. Because of incomplete count data for certain hours, 37 out of the 40 days were used. Count data was provided for each of the standard 13 vehicle classes that run from motorcycles to multi-trailer trucks with seven or more axles. Average daily traffic was 3,583 vehicles, with an average of 472 (13 percent) trucks.

Seasonality was also evaluated as a possible source of bias in the ESAL estimates. ESALs could be either under or overestimated if the count period saw especially high or especially light truck traffic as compared to the rest of the year. However, examination of monthly trucking activity, provided by an oil field trucking support firm, indicated that seasonality was not a factor in use of the road by trucks. Conversions with other truck industry officials also indicated that, at most, seasonality would be a very minor source of bias in our ESAL estimates.

Because the count data is in one direction, equation 5 reduces to:

$$ESAL_i = G_{jt} \times ADDT_i \times 365 \times N_i \times F_{ei} \tag{6}$$

As previously stated, data for Louisiana conditions obtained from the Louisiana DOTD and are reported on truck rather than axle equivalency. The values shown in Table 8 are truck equivalency factors for each of the thirteen vehicle categories. Hence, the variables N_i and F_{Ei} are replaced by one factor, V_i, and the ESAL equation 6 becomes:

$$ESAL_i = G_{jt} \times ADDT_i \times 365 \times V_i \tag{7}$$

Based on the new equation (7), ESAL were calculated for each of the thirteen vehicle classes. The current annual ESAL was estimated to be 160,570. Cumulative ESALs over a twenty year period (a typical road design period) are then estimated under a variety of assumptions about future growth rates. Had the current expansion in the oil and gas activities not occurred in the region, we estimate that the current (1997) annual ESAL would be 134,854 (or 16 percent less than our current estimate).

Assuming a zero growth rate ($G_{jt} = 1$), total cumulative ESAL over 20 years would be 3.2 million. This number of ESAL indicates a need to overlay in 16 years (in the year 2013) for the section of pavement (064021b) with 9.1 inch thickness in the asphalt layer (Table 10 on following page). It indicates a need to be overlay in 12 years (when cumulative ESAL are 2.4 million) for the section (064021a) with the average thickness of 8.1 inches. For the section (064901a) with 6.2 inches of average thickness in the asphalt layer, a need to overlay in five years is indicated (in the year 2002) and for the section (064901b) with an average asphalt layer thickness of 6.0 inches, the estimated need to overlay occurs in the year 2001. Hence, even with no increase in traffic, current projections indicate the need for eventual major rework efforts, with much of that effort occurring in the near future. But a zero growth rate is extremely unrealistic given current increases in truck traffic going into and coming out of Port Fourchon.

Our lowest estimate of the growth rate in truck traffic is based on the assumption that our lower bound estimate of the 1996 to 1997 increase in truck traffic (12 percent)[15] will

---

[15]   See Appendix for the appropriate discussion regarding rate of growth in truck activities in Port Fourchon.

be maintained for three more years through the year 2000 (Table 10). After that date, a two percent growth rate in truck traffic is assumed. Under the lowest growth rate scenario, the 2.3 million ESAL level is predicted to be surpassed in the year 2005 (relating to section 064021a), while the 3.0 million ESAL level (relating to section 064021b) will be surpassed in 2008. For both the 9.2 mile (section 064901a) and 1.7 mile (section 064901b) stretches of road--with average asphalt layer thicknesses of 6.2 inches and 6.0 inches-- the 1.2 million ESAL and 1.1 million ESAL levels are both surpassed in the year 2001. This estimate of ESAL serves as a lower bound estimate of the wear and tear, and need for repavement, for highway 1 due to current and estimated levels of truck traffic.

Table 10: Estimated Year of Repavement, Based on Average Thickness Calculations and ESAL Generated Under Alternative Growth Scenarios							
				Year of Repavement by Growth Scenario			
Road Section	Last Repavement (Year)	Length (Miles)	Mean Thickness (Inches)	No Growth	Low Growth	Medium Growth	High Growth
064021a	1981	5.9	8.13	2009	2006	2004	2004
064021b	1993	7.4	9.08	2013	2008	2007	2005
064901a	1979	9.2	6.21	2002	2001	2001	2000
064901b	1994	1.7	6.02	2001	2001	2000	2000
Source: Louisiana Department of Transportation and Development (DOTD), Baton Rouge, 1997. All road thickness values estimated by DOTD in 1995							

The medium range estimate of the growth rate in truck traffic, is based on an assumption regarding the maintenance of the estimated growth rate in truck traffic from 1996 to 1997. This growth rate has been estimated to range between 12 percent and 24 percent (Table 10). Hence, for the middle range estimate of growth in truck traffic, the medium of the estimates of the 1996 to 1997 increase in truck traffic (18 percent) is assumed to be maintained for three more years (through the year 2000). After that date, a four percent growth rate in truck traffic is assumed. Under the medium growth rate scenario, the 2.3 million ESAL level (section 064021a) is predicted to be surpassed in the year 2004 while the 3.0 million ESAL level (section 064021b) will be surpassed in 2006. The 1.1 million ESAL level (section 064021a) is predicted to be exceeded in the year 2000, while the 1.2 million ESAL level (section 064021b) should be exceeded in the following year.

The highest estimated growth rate is based on the assumption that our upper bound estimate of the 1996 to 1997 increase in truck traffic (24 percent) will be maintained for three more years (through the year 2000). After that date, a five percent growth rate in truck traffic is assumed (Table 10). The five percent annual growth rate is often a standard used by highway departments throughout the U.S. in assessing and prioritizing highway needs. Under the high growth rate scenario, the 2.3 million ESAL level (section

34

064021a) is predicted to be surpassed in the year 2004 while the 3.0 million ESAL level (section 064021b) will be surpassed in 2005. Under the same scenario, the 1.2 million ESAL level (section 064901b) and the 1.1 million ESAL level (section 064901a) are both expected to be exceeded in the year 2000. It is important to note that even the highest growth rate is conservative, in that a five percent growth rate is assumed after the year 2000. Given the growth in the OCS oil and gas activities, it is quite possible that the increase in truck traffic could exceed a five percent growth rate after the year 2000 for at least several years.

A comparison of the estimation concerning when overlays will be needed under the different growth rates is provided in Table 10. Results indicate that different assumptions about the future growth rate in truck traffic did not necessarily result in large changes in the estimates of when repaving must occur. For the section of road (064021b) with an average asphalt layer thickness of 9.1 inches, the estimate ranges from the year 2013, under the no growth scenario, to 2005 under the high growth scenario. For the section of road (064021a) with an average asphalt layer thickness of 8.1 inches, the estimate ranges from the year 2009, under the no growth scenario, to 2004 under the high growth scenario. For the section of road (064901a) with an average asphalt layer thickness of 6.2 inches, the estimate ranges from the year 2002, under the no growth scenario, to 2000 under the high growth scenario. Finally, For the section of road (064901b) with an average asphalt layer thickness of 6.0 inches, the estimate ranges from the year 2001, under the no growth scenario, to 2000 under the high growth scenario.

It is interesting to note the slight difference between the low and high growth rates concerning when overlays must occur (Table 10). For the section of road with the thickest asphalt layer (064021b), the projected difference concerning when overlays must occur is three years (2008 versus 2005). For the sections with average asphalt layer thickness of 8.1 inches (064021a) and 6.2 inches (064901a) the difference between the high and low growth projections is only two years (2006 versus 2004; and 2002 versus 2000). For the section of road with the thinnest layer of asphalt (064901b), the difference in the year of projected repavement between the high and low growth rates is only one year (2001 versus 2000).

A different approach can be taken in evaluating the need to overlay based on differences in asphalt thickness within each of the four sections of Highway 1. That is, traffic bearing capacity is assessed in terms of the individual tenth of a mile increment for the two sections of road. Estimates of when to repave were made by calculating the average of the asphalt layer thickness across each of the 0.1 mile stretch of road, within a given range of asphalt layer thickness. For example, as shown in Table 11 on the following page, the section of road (064901a) was last repaved in 1979 (9.2 miles in length), 21 percent of the road was in the 5 to 6 inch range for asphalt layer thickness and the average thickness of the asphalt layer was 5.6 inches across all 0.1 mile sections in that category.

Table 11: Average Inches and Count of 0.1 Mile Sections by Major Stretch of Road for Highway 1, from Golden Meadow to South of Port Fouchon

Road Section	Last Repave (Year)	Length (Miles)	Average Thickness per Inch Category						
			5-6	6-7	7-8	8-9	9-10	10-11	11-12
064021a	1981	5.9	n/a	6.7	7.6	8.3	9.5	10.3	n/a
064021b	1993	7.4	5.5	6.5	7.8	8.5	9.2	10.5	11.3
064901a	1979	9.2	5.8	6.3	7.1	n/a	n/a	n/a	n/a
064901b	1994	1.7	5.6	6.6	7.2	n/a	n/a	n/a	n/a
Cumulative Count:									
064021a	1981	5.9	0	11	30	45	50	57	
064021b	1993	7.4	1	3	5	45	52	71	74
064901a	1979	9.2	17	79	81				
064901b	1994	1.7	10	16	17				
Cumulative Percentage:									
064021a	1981	5.9	0.0	19.3	52.6	78.9	87.7	100.0	
064021b	1993	7.4	1.4	4.1	6.8	60.8	70.3	95.9	100.0
064901a	1979	9.2	21.0	97.5	100.0				
064901b	1994	1.7	58.8	94.1	100.0				

Note: Total number of evaluated 0.1 mile ons do not equal overall section length in all cases because of bridges or because some portions of the road are concrete with no asphalt overlay.

Dividing each section based on thickness of the asphalt layer for each 0.1 mile increment indicates an earlier time horizon for repaving for the majority of both sections of the road. For example, the majority of section (064021a) has less than 8 inches of pavement. These parts of section 064021a are in need of repaving in 2006 under the zero growth scenario, while the projected year of repaving under the mean scenario is 2009 for the same section (Table 12 on following page). Further, for both the sections that were repaved in 1979 (064901a) and 1994 (064901b), significant percentages of each section (21.0 percent and 58.8 percent) in the 5 to 6 inch category are in need of repavement by the year 2000 under even the low growth scenarios.

Table 12: Estimated Year of Repavement Based on Thickness Calculations and ESAL Generated Under Alternative Growth Scenarios for 0.1 Mile Length Sections of Highway 1 from Golden Meadow to South of Port Fouchon									
Road Section	Growth Scenario	Estimated Repavement Year by Inch Category,							
		5-6	6-7	7-8	8-9	9-10	10-11	11-12	Avg.
064021a	No Growth	n/a	2003	2006	2010	n/o	n/o	n/o	2009
	Low	n/a	2002	2004	2006	2011	2015	n/o	2006
	Medium	n/a	2001	2003	2005	2008	2012	n/o	2004
	High	n/a	2001	2003	2004	2007	2010	n/o	2004
064021b	No Growth	2000	2002	2007	2011	2015	n/o	n/o	2013
	Low	2000	2001	2004	2007	2009	2016	n/o	2008
	Medium	2000	2001	2004	2005	2008	2012	n/o	2007
	High	1999	2000	2003	2004	2006	2010	2015	2005
064901a	No Growth	2001	2002	2005	n/a	n/a	n/a	n/a	2002
	Low	2000	2001	2003	n/a	n/a	n/a	n/a	2001
	Medium	2000	2001	2002	n/a	n/a	n/a	n/a	2001
	High	2000	2000	2002	n/a	n/a	n/a	n/a	2000
064901b	No Growth	2001	2003	2006	n/a	n/a	n/a	n/a	2001
	Low	2000	2001	2003	n/a	n/a	n/a	n/a	2001
	Medium	2000	2001	2004	n/a	n/a	n/a	n/a	2000
	High	2000	2001	2002	n/a	n/a	n/a	n/a	2000

Another approach used in estimating the effect of ESAL on road quality is through changes in surface roughness as measured by the PSI factor. A regression equation provided by Dr. John Metcalf, Professor of Engineering at Louisiana State University, was used to examine the relationship. The equation was based on observed values from an accelerated pavement test on a crushed stone base/asphalt surface pavement in Louisiana. It shows the relationship between road roughness (PSI) and accumulated ESAL. The equation was estimated as:

$$PSI = 5.5 - 0.0025 \ (ESAL X 10^{-3}) \tag{8}$$

$$n = 13 \quad R^2 = 0.91.$$

According to equation 8, the number of ESAL generated in our estimates would result in marked decreases in road quality. For example, the current level of estimated ESAL in 1997 (160,570) would result in a decrease in the PSI of 0.482. Recall that the PSI ranges from 1 (very poor quality) to 5 (excellent quality). Hence, the expected decrease in road quality from even current levels of use (a decline in PSI of 0.482) could lead to significant losses in road quality.

The change in the PSI can also be used in the Rational Factorial Ranking Method (FRM) to indicate the change in this measure of overall highway quality. In the FRM, the PSI is an independent variable and the priority index is the dependent variables. Using the estimated change in PSI under current levels of road use (0.482), the change in overall road quality, as measured by the priority index, can be calculated. The priority index ranges from one for a road of very poor quality to ten for a road of excellent quality.

The calculated priority index under the change in PSI, for each of the sections of road discussed in Table 3 (sections 640101 through 649004), are provided in Table 13 on the following page. The estimated change in the PSI lead to a reduction in the priority index for each of the 27 sections of road of 1.05. The new and original priority index are calculated for the distress factor equal to zero and the distress factor equal to one. Under the original priority index, with the distress factor equal to zero, four sections of road had a priority index value of five, 19 sections had a priority index value of four, and the remaining four sections had a priority index of three. Under the projected priority index (with the change in PSI), and with the distress factor still equal to zero, a marked decline in the condition of highway 1 is apparent. In this case, no sections had a priority index value of five, four sections of road had a priority index of four, 18 sections had a priority index value of three, and the remaining five sections had a priority index of two. For the case when the distress factors equals negative one, the projected decline in the condition of highway 1 is even more apparent. Under the original priority index, with the distress factor now equal to negative one, 12 sections of road had a priority index value of three, and the remaining 15 sections had a priority index value of two. Under the projected priority index (with the change in PSI), and with the distress factor equal to negative one, 11 sections of road had a projected priority index of two, while the remaining 16 sections had a projected priority index of one.

Table 13: Change in Quality of Roads, as Measured by Rational Factorial Ranking Method (FRM)

Road Section	Distress factor equals zero (0)			Distress factor equals negative one (-1)		
	Original	Projected	% Change	Original	Projected	% Change
640101	4.67	3.61	-22.6%	3.01	1.95	-35.1%
640102	4.37	3.31	-24.1%	2.71	1.65	-38.9%
640103	4.39	3.33	-24.0%	2.73	1.67	-38.7%
640104	4.54	3.48	-23.2%	2.88	1.82	-36.7%
640201	4.55	3.50	-23.2%	2.89	1.84	-36.5%
640202	5.25	4.20	-20.1%	3.59	2.54	-29.4%
640501	4.30	3.25	-24.5%	2.64	1.59	-39.9%
640502	3.93	2.87	-26.8%	2.27	1.21	-46.5%
640503	3.93	2.87	-26.8%	2.27	1.21	-46.5%
640504	3.76	2.70	-28.0%	2.10	1.04	-50.2%
640601	4.29	3.24	-24.6%	2.63	1.58	-40.0%
640602	4.00	2.94	-26.4%	2.34	1.28	-45.1%
640603	3.91	2.86	-26.9%	2.25	1.20	-46.8%
640604	4.86	3.81	-21.7%	3.20	2.15	-32.9%
640605	5.09	4.03	-20.7%	3.43	2.37	-30.7%
640701	4.76	3.70	-22.2%	3.10	2.04	-34.0%
640702	5.05	4.00	-20.9%	3.39	2.34	-31.1%
640703	4.90	3.85	-21.5%	3.24	2.19	-32.5%
640704	5.15	4.10	-20.5%	3.49	2.44	-30.2%
640705	4.83	3.78	-21.8%	3.17	2.12	-33.2%
640801	4.14	3.09	-25.5%	2.48	1.43	-42.5%
640802	4.82	3.76	-21.9%	3.16	2.10	-33.4%
640803	4.96	3.90	-21.3%	3.30	2.24	-32.0%
649001	4.33	3.27	-24.4%	2.67	1.61	-39.5%
649002	4.18	3.12	-25.2%	2.52	1.46	-41.9%
649003	4.33	3.27	-24.4%	2.67	1.61	-39.5%
649004	4.85	3.80	-21.7%	3.19	2.14	-33.0%

Note: Change in PSI equals 0.4817, based on the estimated marginal effect of current estimated annual EASL.

V. CONCLUSION

Due to a combination of several favorable factors, interest in deepwater activities in the Central Gulf of Mexico has been exceedingly high in recent years. Because of this increased interest, concern has been expressed regarding the ability of LA 1 to "adequately" handle the expected increase in traffic associated with the increased offshore activities. In general, this ability entails two dimensions: (a) a congestion (i.e., capacity) dimension and (b) a deterioration dimension.

The overall purpose of this study was to examine these two dimensions in relation to increased economic activities associated with deepwater oil-and-gas development. The study, in general, suggests that concern is likely warranted. With respect to the issue of capacity, analysis of historical data suggest that ADT growth rates from three percent to six percent per year may be forthcoming as deepwater activities expand. Within this range of ADT annual growth, the level of service provided by LA 1 will decline significantly. As such, the ability of LA 1 to provide an "adequate" level of services needed to support expanding offshore oil-and-gas activities will become increasingly strained.

The study also suggests that deterioration of LA 1 will also be exacerbated with expanding oil-and-gas activities. Specifically, expansion in these activities during the past few years was found to result in a significantly higher amount of truck traffic into and out of Port Fourchon and additional increases in truck traffic are anticipated in association with expansion of offshore activities. The increased truck traffic, and future increases, has and will continue to result in more rapid deterioration of LA 1 and, hence, the need for more frequent pavement rehabilitation.

VI. ACKNOWLEDGEMENTS

The authors would like to thank all those who assisted with the different aspects of this report. In particular, appreciation is extended to the staff at DODT who graciously provided the authors with much of the historical road usage data and to several of the trucking companies who service the Port Fourchon area. Some of these companies provided detailed records of activities which greatly facilitated completion of this report. Finally, a note of special thanks is extended to Dr. John Metcalf, Chaired Professor of Engineering, Louisiana State University.

References

Walls, M.A. 1994. "Using a 'Hybrid' Approach to Model Oil and Gas Supply: A Case Study of the Gulf of Mexico Outer Continental Shelf." Land Economics, 70(1):1-19.

Melancon, J.M., C.L. Nixdorff, R.C. Bowser, and C. Yu. 1997. "Gulf of Mexico Outer Continental Shelf Daily Oil and Gas Production Rate Projections From 1996 Through 2000." U.S. Department of the Interior, Minerals Management Service, Gulf of Mexico OCS Regional Office.

Cranswick, D. and J. Regg. 1997. "Deepwater in the Gulf of Mexico: America's New Frontier." U.S. Department of the Interior, Minerals Management Service, Gulf of Mexico OCS Region.

Anonymous. 1997. "Born -Again Basin Attracts Flurry of Activity." Petroleum Economist (January)

McKenzie, L.S., III, P.J. Xander, M.T.C. Johnson, B. Baldwin, and D.W. Davis. 1993. *Socioeconomic Impacts of Declining Outer Continental Shelf Oil and Gas Activities in the Gulf of Mexico.* OCS Study MMS 93-0028. U.S. Department of the Interior, Minerals Management Service, Gulf of Mexico OCS Region, New Orleans, Lousiana. 240pp.

Appendix

To determine the average annual growth in truck traffic in and out of Port Fourchon, the major for-hire trucking firms that serviced the port area, as well as other independent truck firms out of the Houston area, were surveyed. These trucking firms were asked to provide information pertaining to annual change in Port Fourchon operations during the 1994-97 period as well as the absolute number of trucks within a given time frame in 1997. In some instances, firms provided actual records for all or part of the 1994-97 period. Firms unable (or unwilling) to provide actual records were asked to estimate growth and the absolute level of activities for a specific period of time within the 1997 year.

Among firms surveyed, growth between 1994 and 1995 was estimated to equal 13%. Between 1995 and 1996, growth was estimated to equal 18%. Finally, growth between 1996 and 1997 was estimated to equal 24%. These growth rate estimates, however, should be considered "upper bound" for two reasons. First, only the trucking firms known to service oil-and-gas activities were surveyed. Specifically, trucking firms servicing, say, the seafood industry operating out of Port Fourchon were not surveyed. To the extent that trucking firms not surveyed had smaller (or even negative) growth rates, the estimates provided above should be considered as "liberal".

The second reason for considering the above estimates as "upper bound" reflects the fact that not all trucks traversing Highway 1 in the port area are destined to enter the port. For example, many of the trucks may be servicing the Grand Isle area. In general, the majority of the trucks servicing the Grand Isle area are probably not related to oil-and-gas activities and, as such, there may have been little growth in this segment during the 19943-97 period.

As a result of these two factors, a "lower bound" estimate of growth rate during the 1994-97 period was also calculated. This "lower bound" estimate was derived by determining the proportion of trucks identified in the survey in relation to the total number of trucks identified by the counter data. In general the identified trucks represented approximately 40% of the total number of trucks reported from the counter data. To establish a "lower bound" estimate, the growth rate with respect to the proportion of trucks not identified was set equal to zero. Using this method, the lower bound estimate of growth between 1994 and 1995 was found to equal five percent. Between 1995 and 1996, the lower bound estimate of growth equaled eight percent. Finally, the lower bound estimate of growth between 1996 and 1997 equaled 11%.

The Department of the Interior Mission

As the Nation's principal conservation agency, the Department of the Interior has responsibility for most of our nationally owned public lands and natural resources. This includes fostering sound use of our land and water resources; protecting our fish, wildlife, and biological diversity; preserving the environmental and cultural values of our national parks and historical places; and providing for the enjoyment of life through outdoor recreation. The Department assesses our energy and mineral resources and works to ensure that their development is in the best interests of all our people by encouraging stewardship and citizen participation in their care. The Department also has a major responsibility for American Indian reservation communities and for people who live in island territories under U.S. administration.

The Minerals Management Service Mission

As a bureau of the Department of the Interior, the Minerals Management Service's (MMS) primary responsibilities are to manage the mineral resources located on the Nation's Outer Continental Shelf (OCS), collect revenue from the Federal OCS and onshore Federal and Indian lands, and distribute those revenues.

Moreover, in working to meet its responsibilities, the **Offshore Minerals Management Program** administers the OCS competitive leasing program and oversees the safe and environmentally sound exploration and production of our Nation's offshore natural gas, oil and other mineral resources. The MMS **Minerals Revenue Management** meets its responsibilities by ensuring the efficient, timely and accurate collection and disbursement of revenue from mineral leasing and production due to Indian tribes and allottees, States and the U.S. Treasury.

The MMS strives to fulfill its responsibilities through the general guiding principles of: (1) being responsive to the public's concerns and interests by maintaining a dialogue with all potentially affected parties and (2) carrying out its programs with an emphasis on working to enhance the quality of life for all Americans by lending MMS assistance and expertise to economic development and environmental protection.

www.ingramcontent.com/pod-product-compliance
Lightning Source LLC
Chambersburg PA
CBHW052008280526
45793CB00005B/901